PETRA

"OBLIQUE" TAKEN FROM A HEIGHT OF ABOUT 4,500 FEET ABOVE THE CITY, LOOKING FROM EAST TO WEST. IN THE FOREGROUND ARE THE CULTIVATED TERRACES OF ALJI. THE SITE OF THE CITY CROSSES THE CENTRE OF THE PICTURE FROM RIGHT TO LEFT, THE DRY WHITE BED OF THE WADI MUSA AND THE QASR-AL-BINT BEING VISIBLE. BEYOND THE CITY THE WESTERN RANGE, BACKED BY J. ATUD AND THE DISTANT GHOR. AT THE EXTREME LEFT J. HARUN IS JUST VISIBLE.

PETRA
ITS HISTORY
AND MONUMENTS

BY

SIR ALEXANDER B. W. KENNEDY
LL.D., F.R.S., F.R.G.S.

"They say the Lion and the Lizard keep
The Courts where Jamshyd gloried and drank deep :
And Bahrám, that great Hunter—the Wild Ass
Stamps o'er his Head, but cannot break his Sleep."

Omar Khayyam.

1925
LONDON
COUNTRY LIFE
20 TAVISTOCK STREET, COVENT GARDEN

Printed in Great Britain

PREFACE

THE rediscovery of the remains of the rock-carved City of Petra was made in 1812 by a young Swiss acting under the auspices (and presumably at the expense) of an English Archæological or Geographical Society, and the first records of his discovery were published, in English, in 1822. His visit, unfortunately, lasted only a few hours, so that he had little opportunity of seeing the place. Perhaps the most complete account of Petra which has been yet published in English is still that of two naval officers (Irby and Mangles) who spent several days there in 1818, and published their journal (for private circulation) a century ago, in 1823. Since then I am afraid it must be confessed that the many English and American visitors who have published their stories have been interested so entirely in matters other than those archæological that, apart from the identification, from time to time, of several places of cult, they have really done next to nothing to indicate to us the general nature of the wonderful place they had visited. It has been left to the industry and thoroughness of various European professors within the last thirty years to make anything approaching to a real exploration of Petra, and their explorations have yielded invaluable results. These results, however, have been published only in German, and the works in which they are contained are now mostly out of print and very difficult to obtain, besides which they cover an inconveniently large number of huge volumes.

Even the least scientifically minded—or the most philistine—of the visitors have obviously felt the extraordinary fascination of the place itself. To me this fascination was so great that I accepted with enthusiasm an invitation to a prolonged visit to the Amir Abdullah's camp there in 1923, during which I was able to arrange for another long visit in the year following. As a result of these visits I have thought it worth while to write this book, in which my object has been to draw, in general outline, as clear and complete a picture as I can of Petra itself, with its monuments, in the hope of sufficiently interesting English visitors, and above all English explorers, to induce some of them to take up the still unsolved problems of the place—problems which I feel to be none the less inviting that old age and poor health make it impossible for me to attempt to tackle them myself. This must be my apologia for the following pages.

It was by the good offices of Mr. H. St.J. B. Philby (at that time Chief British Representative in Trans-Jordan) that I was enabled to make a first short visit to Petra in 1922, and my long visits in each of the two following years were also rendered possible by the arrangements which he was able to make, and especially by his ability to secure the approval and good will of His Highness the Amir Abdullah and of His Majesty King Husain. In 1923 I had the pleasure of being a guest at the Amir's camp in Petra, and in 1923 I received from King Husain, in his camp at Shunet Nimrim, a very cordial permission, of which I took full advantage, to establish my own camp and invite my own guests at Petra.

I hoped to have been able to persuade Mr. Philby to take the responsibility of co-authorship with me in this book, but, unfortunately for me, he did not see his way to this. He has been kind enough, however, to help me very greatly in its production, and is, in fact, the author of the whole of the first and most important chapter, which covers the especially geographical part of the story, as well as special explorations which he made both north and south of the site of the City. His official duties in Trans-Jordan took him repeatedly over the ground, and there is no one living who has a more intimate knowledge of it than he has. I was, therefore, specially fortunate in being able to persuade him to deal with this part of the subject.

Mr. Philby has also kindly taken the responsibility for the transliteration of the Arabic place-names, except in the one matter that I have (under protest from the Arabic scholar) refused to burden my pages with diacritical marks. These naturally convey no meaning except to the elect, and (as I have found from experience during the last two years) they are most irritating when they occur in a text in a European language. I must piously hope that Oriental scholars who stoop to read the book will forgive me for the sake of the majority of readers who are not so qualified.

On the surface of the ground at Petra practically nothing is to be found but Roman remains—fragments of pottery and occasional coins of no very great interest. But the great rock-carved monuments which are the glory of the place are at least six or seven centuries older than the Roman occupation of the City, and we know that at least for the latter part of this time there existed in the *Wadi Musa*, as Strabo tells us, a Nabataean City of built houses. In the carved rocks we have only very vague traces of the religious cult of these people. Below the Roman surface layer there ought probably to be found more detailed indications of Nabataean worship, and possibly below these again some signs of still older culture. Innumerable inhabitants, also, must surely have been buried within the precincts of the city, and traces of these burials also remain to be found. Up to the present time, however, permission to dig on the site of the City has been refused by the Arabian authorities, so that nothing has been done in this direction. I was fortunate enough to obtain from Mr. A. J. B. Wace, when he returned from Athens, the promise that he would come out with me in 1924 in order to make at least preliminary investigation with a view to finding what probability there was of archæological discovery if the work were to be systematically carried out. The promise was, of course, conditional on the necessary permission being obtained from the King. It is quite possible that this permission might eventually have been obtained, but unfortunately before King Husain had completed the difficult process of making up his mind Mr. Wace had cabled to me from America that engagements there made it impossible for him to get to Petra in time. I hope that some future explorer may find the Fates more propitious.

During my visit in 1923 an airplane survey of the site of the City was made, a part of which was reproduced in the *Journal of the Royal Geographical Society* for April, 1924, in connection with a paper which I read before the Society. I was able to persuade the Air Ministry here to allow me to have a more extensive survey made while I was in camp in 1924, and the result of this later survey is given in the reproduction of the Mosaic (covering about fifty square miles of country) in this volume. In connection with this matter I have to thank the Air Ministry and its officials for the hearty way in which they supported the scheme, and especially Squadron Leaders Laws and Graham, as well as Major Bullock (the Secretary to the Air Minister). General Tudor was in command at Bir Salem when the work was arranged for in 1923 and 1924, and was succeeded during its progress by Colonel Hector Reid. Group Captain M. D. K. McEwen, who was C.O. at Amman, took an especially active interest in the necessary arrangements, and particularly in the formation of the necessary aeroplane quarters at Anaiza. The actual observers (two planes were used) were Flight-Lieutenant Wm. Elliot, D.F.C. (who was unfortunately called back to headquarters soon after the start), Flying Officers John Marsden (in charge), C. J. Collingwood and H. N. Thornton, and Sergeant-Major Haug. These gentlemen (all of the 14th Squadron R.A.F.) took the keenest personal interest in the work, and the result, as indicated by the Mosaic (which was put together for me at Farnborough), is certainly of unique and permanent value. In the 1923 air survey the pilot in charge was Flight-Lieutenant Sorley, also of the 14th Squadron.

In addition to the vertical exposures which constitute the Mosaic, a number of " obliques " were taken, several of which I am glad to be able to reproduce. These views give an extraordinarily vivid idea of the rugged nature of the district.

The vertical photographs were taken from a height of about 8,000 feet above Qasr' al Bint, with a lens of $8\frac{1}{4}$ inches focus. The obliques were taken from a height about 3,500 feet lower, and with a lens of $10\frac{1}{4}$ inches focus. All the plates used were 5 by 4 inches. The 1923 photographs were taken from about 5,000 feet above the City, so that their scale is much larger than that of the later survey.

The determination of the scale of the airplane survey, in the absence of any satisfactory control points, has been far from easy. I owe this determination, as well as the preparation of the index map by which the use of the survey has been greatly facilitated, to Mr. H. F. Milne, of the staff of the Royal Geographical Society. Our measured base was only a short one, but it was connected up by theodolite triangulation with a number of identifiable points at considerable distances. The result has been to show that although Brünnow's map is substantially correct as regards its general topography, the scale which has been marked upon it is entirely erroneous, and makes distances measured upon it somewhere about 35 per cent. too great. As to their contours, of course, Brünnow's maps are entirely imaginary.

Since the text was in type my attention has been called to the work of Herr Theodor Wiegand* and his colleagues at Petra in 1916, published four years ago. This party of archæologists spent a fortnight camping in the chambers of the Khazna with the special object of examining and interpreting such ruins of the Roman City as are still left. In the result they have been able to make a reconstruction of the central part of this City far more detailed than anything which has hitherto been attempted. Incidentally Herr Wiegand discusses at length the probable age of the Khazna itself, and I understand him—basing his conclusions entirely upon stylistic data—to arrive at the result that its pre-Augustan Greco-Roman details cannot possibly have been copied so late as the second century A.D., to which period he assigns the Florentinus tomb. He therefore dates the Khazna rather in Augustan times—*i.e.*, long before the Roman occupation.

Assuming that his conclusions are justified, they would indicate definitely that the Khazna could not have been constructed *anywhere* before that date, but I do not think they prove, although he seems to take this for granted, that it actually must have been constructed at that time at Petra, however possible this might have been. On grounds of a more general nature than the mere architectural style, which I have dealt with in the text, I am still inclined to give the building a much later date. I am afraid the matter must be left uncertain; I am unable myself, at any rate, to formulate any dogmatic conclusion.

Wiegand's examination revealed the existence of a second (smaller) market-place west of the great forum (p. 60), the site of which is quite visible on the 1923 airplane map. He also discovered the site of a second (smaller) theatre in the outer Siq.

Wiegand gives a reconstruction—in plan and elevation—of the line of the probable roadway into the Siq from the East, and the method by which the water in the Wadi Musa was diverted northwards under a bridge to the tunnel, which is very illuminating and which explains several

---

* *Wissenschaftliche Veröffentlichen des Deutsch-Türkischen Denkmalschutz-Commandos* (Heft III., " Petra "), edited by Theodor Wiegand. Berlin, 1921.

points which have hitherto remained difficult to understand, including the probable use of the great arch in the Siq (see p. 61).

Wiegand's party discovered, during this survey, the perplexing error in the scale of Brünnow's maps to which I refer below. He also develops at some length a theory which appears to me quite unnecessary, and even fanciful, for the progressive development of the Nabataean monuments. I hardly think he would have suggested this theory if his stay at Petra had allowed him to give anything like the attention to these monuments which he has given so successfully to the Roman ruins.

I am indebted to my friends Mr. Philby, Mr. A. L. Mumm (who was in camp during the whole of the 1924 expedition), and Sir Aurel Stein, for the use of a large number of the negatives which are here reproduced. I have noted these in the Index to the Illustrations. I am also indebted to Messrs. Vester and Co. (Jerusalem) for permission to reproduce four photographs taken by the photographers of the American Colony. I am also very much indebted to Mr. Ewart Millar for his work in reducing, enlarging, and in some cases reproducing the negatives.

It may interest photographers to know that a considerable number of my own photographs here reproduced in postcard size and larger were taken with a Dallmeyer " Speed " Camera on films only $2\frac{1}{4}$ by $1\frac{1}{2}$ inches. I think it will be found that the slight additional softness due to the enlargement is not, on the whole, a drawback.

I am indebted to the Royal Geographical Society for permission to use the general map (Amman to Aqaba) facing p. 1. I have to thank my brother, Mr. Wardlaw Kennedy (late of Haileybury), for all the classical translations. To my experienced friend Miss Jean Kennedy I am indebted for the very carefully prepared Index.

I must certainly, also, not omit to mention Mr. B. G. Treverton, on whom devolved the troublesome work of making and carrying through all arrangements for a long and extensive camping in 1924, including the engagements and paying of all the Arabs concerned; and also Mr. Kirkbride of C.B.R.'s office at Amman for much assistance in connection with the same matters.

With reference to the remarks on p. 4 regarding the political status of the Petra district, it has to be noted that the greater part of the Ma'an province (including Petra itself) was in July last (since Chapter I was in type) annexed by the British Government to the territory subject to the Palestine Mandate. King Husain was at the same time removed from Aqaba to Cyprus.

ERRATA

On p. 9, line 2, *for* 4280 *read* 4430, and *for* highest *read* lowest.
On p. 50, line 18 from bottom, *for* Tarfani *read* Wastani.
The titles of figures 181 and 183 have unfortunately been transposed. See pp. 71 and 72.

CONTENTS

CHAPTER I

PETRA AND ITS SURROUNDINGS—GENERAL DESCRIPTION

CHAPTER II

CHAPTER III

CHAPTER IV

THE MONUMENTS OF PETRA

CHAPTER V

THE NORTH-EASTERN REGION

CHAPTER VI

CHAPTER VII

CHAPTER VIII

LIST OF ILLUSTRATIONS

PLATES

FRONTISPIECE.—" Oblique " taken from a height of about 4,500 feet above the City, looking from east to west. In the foreground are the cultivated terraces of Alji. The site of the City crosses the centre of the picture from right to left, the dry white bed of the Wadi Musa and the Qasr al Bint being visible. Beyond the City the western range, backed by Jabal Atud and the distant Ghor. At the extreme left Jabal Harun is just visible.

PLATE I.—" Oblique " looking up the site of the City from north to south between the western range (on right) and the Khubdha mass on left, with the outlet of the Siq. The Nasara rocks are in the centre in the foreground.

PLATE II.—" Oblique " of Jabal Harun (Mount Hor) taken from north to south over the mountains of the western wall. (See Chapter I., p. 9).

PLATE III.—" Oblique " showing a hitherto unknown Wadi to the south-east of the City. (See pp. 19 and 82).

FIGURES

The negatives of the figures marked P. were taken by Mr. Philby, those marked M. by Mr. A. L. Mumm, those marked S. by Sir Aurel Stein. The Figures marked V. are from negatives taken by the American Colony photographer, and are reproduced here by the kind permission of Messrs. Vester and Co., Jerusalem. The rest of the negatives were taken by the Author.

MAPS.

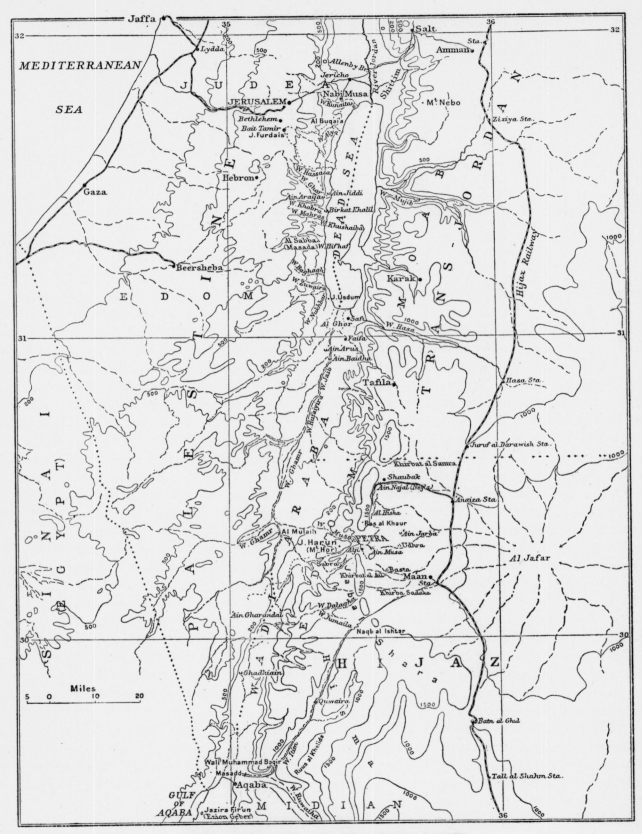

GENERAL MAP OF PETRA AND SURROUNDING COUNTRY.

(*Heights in Metres.*)

PETRA

CHAPTER I
GENERAL DESCRIPTION OF PETRA AND ITS SURROUNDINGS

I.—INTRODUCTORY

(See Map opposite, and the Air-Plane Maps.)

THE Syrian Hamad or North Arabian Desert—the desert to the northward of the great sand-barrier which almost encircles the central core of Arabia—rises steadily and almost imperceptibly from the alluvial flats of Mesopotamia and the northern shores of the Persian Gulf to a mean height of some 3,000 feet above sea-level along the line of the Hijaz Railway. The western part of this great desert is mainly of Cretaceous formation with occasional traces of later geological epochs—*e.g.*, in the depression of Wadi Sirhan and the volcanic tract of Jabal Druz with its southward outliers—and scattered " islands " of what may provisionally be regarded as Nubian sandstone at Jauf, for instance, and in the Tubaik ridge. Westward of the Hijaz Railway, as the Rift Valley is approached, the Cretaceous surface rises more steeply to a long ridge with a mean elevation of 5,000 feet above sea-level, which forms the spine, as it were, of Edom and Moab. From its crest one looks out over the great trough of the Rift Valley (see Frontispiece), beyond which the Cretaceous limestone of the eastern desert is continued in the uplands of Palestine. The continuity of this Cretaceous surface is, however, broken along the eastern fringe of the rift by two important features, two parallel ranges of insignificant width and, for the present, of unascertained length, which have apparently never at any time in their history been covered by the sea. The western of the two ranges is of Archean granite with veins of porphyry, basalt, and other constituents—the mountain range of Midian, whose most northerly known point lies but a short distance westward of Petra in a ridge of porphyry, and which extends southward along the coasts of the Gulf of Aqaba and the Red Sea to a point not yet definitely determined. Eastward of it, intervening between it and the Cretaceous desert, is the second range—a narrow strip of Nubian sandstone, which, beginning as a land surface at the southern extremity of the Dead Sea, runs southward to the latitude of Madaïn Salih and Madina and probably further. This sandstone tract is of terrestrial formation, due, we may suppose, to weathering of the granite mountains to the west, whose rugged and fantastic crags it imitates and even surpasses in the strange wildness of its outlines. Where the two are near enough to each other to be seen together, as, for instance, in the Quwaira plain between Ma'an and Aqaba it is difficult to distinguish them by eye with any certainty—they present the same shapes and colours. The one is, indeed, the child of the other, and it is only on a close approach to them that one discerns the features of the parent to be coarse, wrinkled, and seared with age, those of the offspring to be soft and tinted with all the bloom of youth.

The juxtaposition of these two barriers, of granite and sandstone respectively, athwart the lines of communication between the various cradles of the human race—between Egypt on the one hand and Syria, Mesopotamia, and Southern Arabia on the other—at a time when maritime enterprise was still hesitant and fearful, forced man in his infancy to seek a way through them; and a glance at the map will suffice to show that, geographically, Petra was ideally situated to form a clearing-house for the commerce of the world as it then was. The land-route from Southern Arabia *via* Mecca to the countries of the Mediterranean was all-important for the supply of the luxuries of life—spices, gold and precious stones, apes and peacocks—which the rapid development of civilisation demanded; and thus it was that, perhaps about the sixth century B.C., Petra began to establish a position as a cosmopolitan emporium, which it retained for about a thousand years.

The geographical claim of this locality was reinforced by the circumstance that Nature had by its tectonic activities endowed it in abundance with the one commodity essential then as now to all human enterprise—namely, water. And not only had it endowed it with water, but had so arranged its physical configuration as to provide man, subject to effort and exertion on his part, with a reservoir in which to store it for the purpose of securing a regular supply at all times. The lofty Cretaceous ridge on the east at this point describes a wide semicircle, whose arc, with horns thrust out westward towards Wadi Araba, is subtended by a double chord consisting of two parallel folds of the Nubian sandstone running roughly N.N.W. and S.S.E. with a mile-wide space between them, whose northern and southern ends are so tilted upwards as to form a basin. Into the space included between the more easterly sandstone ridge and that part of the arc which it subtends pour the torrent-waters engendered by the snows which regularly during the winter fall upon the Cretaceous ridge, and the perennial rivulets issuing from numerous springs in its western flank. The two main channels are Wadi al Jamal descending from Ras al Hatti, and Wadi Musa coming from the heights of al Rasif further north and containing the source known as Ain Musa, or the spring of Moses. These channels join at a point below the terraced orchards of Alji village (Fig. 1), now the only habitation in the district, under the name of Wadi Musa, and from this point they pour their waters into the central basin of Petra itself through a number of narrow canyons, in all probability created not by water-erosion, but by the cracking of the sandstone fold in different directions. The most important of these is the famous gorge of al Siq, which in the heyday of Petra's prosperity was paved to form the ceremonial entrance to the city; it was provided on either side with piped aqueducts to carry such part of the water as was not diverted through the tunnel of al Mudhlim (Fig. 194) to find its way into the Petra basin after confluence at a point known as Sidd al Ma'ajin with the contents of other canyons—Wadi Mudhlim, Maqaris al Sulaib and Sha'ib al Qais (in that order from west to east)—round the northern extremity of the eastern or Khubdha ridge. A canyon, somewhat broader than that of al Siq and known as al Siyagh, similarly cleaves the western sandstone fold and forms the only exit for the waters accumulated in the central basin, which it leads out through a narrow cleft (Fig. 2) in a tongue of porphyry lying athwart its path to a steep fall close under the northern shoulder of Jabal Atud into the Araba valley below. It will be seen from this description that a little human ingenuity would suffice to secure an ample water-supply within the Petra basin. Signs are not wanting that such ingenuity was, indeed, exercised in full measure, and to it Petra, which provided its settlers with easily-worked building-material and with the inspiration to build grandly therewith, owed the glory and pre-eminence which it enjoyed for a millennium under its Nabataean rulers and the eagle of Imperial Rome.

As before its rise, so, since its fall some fifteen centuries ago, the uncouth children of Edom, tending their flocks amid the crags and valleys of Mount Seir, have with indolent apathy watched the life-giving waters of the Vale of Moses course by through the ruinous remnants of a once-great city into the desert sands below. Long since have they rifled the tombs of a by-gone age of such valuable articles as may have been placed in them in honour of the dead, while of more recent years they have discovered a modest profit even in the worthless pots and sherds of the ancients, which they sell for small sums to the tourist from Europe and America, to whom, in addition, they act for a small consideration as guides. For the rest the children of Edom have changed but little in three thousand years. The scanty orchards of Alji are all that survive in a district noted in its prime for the abundance of its fruit-trees and vineyards; the people are, as they were, shepherds roaming with their sheep and goats in an area, limited in extent but jealously guarded as of yore against all intrusion from outside. Their *Shaikhs* surround themselves in modest state with a following of twenty to thirty tents—seldom more; while everywhere, wherever there may be a puddle or small pool of water, one may come across individual families with no more than a tent or two eking out a sorry existence in the rugged wilderness of crag and rock. The children run naked or clad in the merest rags; the women go unveiled in draggling garments; the men for the most part wear no more than a head-kerchief and a dirty smock reaching to the knee and girt at the waist with a cartridge belt—they invariably carry a rifle, for modern rifles are cheap enough in these parts since the War. Such, completed by a " trinity " of tooth-pick, ear-pick, and tweezers to extract thorns from the feet, is their accoutrement, and such, less the firearms, it must have been since the beginning of time. Their one occupation in life being to exist in face of the odds pitted against them by Nature and their fellow-men, it is not surprising that they should be suspicious and grasping; but they have in large measure that good-humour and geniality of disposition which seem to result from a life of hardship and privation under primitive conditions and which display themselves only after the reserve, with which the stranger is invariably received, has thawed off, as it always does if the stranger is mild and his presence within their gates likely to be profitable to them. Bread and water and milk form the simple diet of these poor folk, with raisins, pomegranates, and figs on occasion. Their only luxury is tobacco, which the men smoke in earthen pipes, whose accumulated nicotine-impregnated residue the women pick out to ruminate or stuff into the interstices between their teeth—a disgusting habit.

The modern occupants of the Wadi Musa district, as it is officially styled, belong to a small semi-independent tribe called Liyathina (Fig. 3), which is subdivided into four distinct sections, namely:

1. Shurur under two *Shaikhs*, Musa al Mughannin and Falah ibn Sa'id;
2. Farjat also under two *Shaikhs*, Dhaifallah ibn Muhammad and Ali ibn Isa;
3. Alaya under Mu'ammar ibn Bashir; and
4. Ubaidiya under two *Shaikhs*, Khalil al Awar and Muhammad al Hasan.

The Liyathina* have no very clear idea of their origins and history but, like the neighbouring tribe of Na'aimat (subdivided into three sections—namely, Salamat, Salalima, and Alaïda), which enjoys a prescriptive right of tillage in a considerable area on the eastern slope of the main Cretaceous ridge, known as al Shara (*i.e.*, Mount Seir), have undoubted affinities, whether of blood or merely feudal dependence, with their powerful eastern neighbours, the Huwaitat tribe, which occupies the north-western corner of Arabia and is represented by offshoots in the Sinai peninsula and even in Egypt. This tribe is split up into several sections quite independent of each other, but, so far as Petra is in question, we are concerned only with one of them, the important section of Jawazi, which, under its well-known and powerful *Shaikh*, Hamad ibn Jazi, ranges northwards from Ma'an to Tafila. Hamad, in virtue of some unrecorded right, exercises a vague authority over both Na'aimat and

---

* Burton, in *The Gold Mines of Midian*, p. 323, notes the opinion of a Dr. Wilson and others that "the Liyasina (from Lais, the lion of Judah ?) are Simeonites or other Bene-Israel," and also Professor Palmer's view that "these unmitigated scoundrels 'retain not only the distinctive physiognomy, but many of the customs of the Jews, such as wearing the Pharisaic lovelocks.' " Compare also Laianites mentioned by Diodorus as noted by Burton, *ibid.*, p. 180.

Liyathina, but the latter never explicitly admit the fact, though they implicitly recognise it at suitable seasons by the tendering of presents to an overlord, any tendency on whose part to interfere within the confines of the Petra district with their effective independence would be resented and resisted by force of arms.

The Liyathina are, therefore, in effect masters in their own house. Under the Turkish régime they paid revenue to the central government in the desultory fashion which satisfied the official dignity of that government in the more inaccessible parts of its dominions. Wadi Musa formed a subdistrict, or *Mudiriya*, of the Ma'an district of the Province of Syria, but since the end of the War it has, with the neighbouring subdistricts of Shaubak, Aqaba, and Tabuk, been loosely included in the new kingdom of the Hijaz, and nominally governed by the *Qaïm-Maqam*, or district-governor of Ma'an. In fact, no attempt was made until the autumn of 1923 to introduce any kind of regular administration into this group of subdistricts, whose inhabitants, therefore, enjoyed, from 1918 to 1923 inclusive, the privilege of paying no taxes. At the end of 1923, however, this state of affairs was brought to an end by the appointment of Sharif Marzuq ibn Tukhaimi to the governorship of Ma'an (Fig. 4), with instructions to set up a regular administration in each of the subdistricts referred to. He addressed himself to his task with remarkable tact and considerable success—the result, so far as the Petra district is concerned, being the appointment of one of the Liyathina *Shaikhs*, Muhammad al Hasan, as *Mudir* of the district and the creation under his control of a locally-recruited gendarmerie, some twenty strong, at the expense of the government treasury. It was expected that in due course the next step—the collection of revenue—would become feasible and, on the occasion of King Husain's visit to Ma'an in the spring of 1924, that district was officially raised to the status of a province, or *Wilayat*, with Ghalib Pasha al Sha'lan as *Wali* and Commander-in-Chief of a considerable garrison. The Wahhabi attack on Mecca in the latter part of 1924, and the resulting abdication of King Husain, who betook himself by sea to Aqaba and spent the days of his exile partly at that place and partly at Ma'an, has doubtless checked such progress as was expected to result from these administrative changes, and a tentative suggestion was recently made by the British Government to the new King of the Hijaz, Ali ibn Husain, that the Ma'an province should be transferred to Trans-Jordan as part of the territory under British mandate for its greater security against Wahhabi attacks. This proposal was, however, not palatable to King Ali, and has apparently not been further pressed. Petra, therefore, remains a part of Hijaz territory, as it has been since the War.

From that portion of the Hijaz Railway which lies between Ma'an and Anaiza stations the country westward as far as the line of the Roman *Limes* is a vast desert plain thickly covered with low scrub of the scented wild-sage (*Shih*), which provides excellent pasturage for the camels of the Huwaitat. The wild-rhubarb (*Kahmum*) abounds throughout this tract, as also a large and beautiful dark-coloured iris and a small fibrous bulb known as *Shuhum*, which in spring-time forms a common article of food—both raw and cooked—among the local people. Bustard are common everywhere, land-tortoises are frequently met with, and occasional gazelle visit this area, which, except for seasonal torrents coursing down from the hills to the desert, is entirely waterless. Occasional outcrops of basalt rock and patches of scattered lava here and there diversify the monotonous Cretaceous surface.

The Roman *Limes*, which is easily traceable from far to the north by its ruined settlements, occasional milestones singly or in groups, patches of basalt pavement and the remains of more elaborate *Castra*, runs in this tract along the base of the eastern slope of the Shara range, where, as might be expected, water emerges at the surface in the form of springs from the flanks of the three ridges which constitute this mountain. The *Limes*, leaving the important position of Shaubak to the west, crosses what is now the regular motor-track between Anaiza station and Petra at the spring of Ain Najal (the Roman station of Negla), where there is ample water in a spring and running stream in a narrow valley trending eastward between low ridges, on which at several points traces of ancient habitations still exist, and flint* implements, generally of inferior type, may be found in plenty.   Hence the *Limes* runs southward to two springs called Jarba, beyond which, at no great distance, it reaches the important and imposing *Castrum* of Udhra.†   This must have been a very important *point d'appui* in the Roman scheme of political penetration towards the spice-lands. Its ruins are of massive masonry, whose outline is easily traceable—the walls and gates, and bastions of an impregnable fortress of considerable extent.   The buildings within the fortified circuit have suffered from the ravages of time more than the wall itself, but there are numerous remnants of barrel-vaulted structures, and the depredations of the Huwaitat *Shaikhs*, who have built themselves houses here in the midst of a considerable tract of cultivation dependent on the copious water issuing from several springs, have made but little impression on the work of the Roman engineers.

From Udhra the Roman road runs southward, always along the base of the mountain, past the springs of Basta and Khirbat al Ail and several others, to Khirba Sadaka, an extensive but seldom-visited group of ruins of massive masonry with much broken pottery scattered about its surface—obviously another *Castrum*, though probably not so important as that of Udhra, or perhaps less kindly treated by time.   Beyond to the southward a series of springs with traces of ancient ruins in their neighbourhood lead to the main road between Ma'an and Aqaba at the springs of Abal Lisan, whence the main ridge may be crossed by the pass of Naqb al Ishtar—practicable now even for heavy motor-traffic.

Between the tract just described and the sandstone ridges which contain Petra lies the main range of al Shara (Mount Seir) rising from the *Limes* in a series of three ridges of progressively increasing height to its summit 5,000 feet (and in places more than that) above sea-level.

The northern part of this range within the district under consideration—namely, from Shaubak to Petra—is, or rather was, covered by an extensive forest of stunted oak and terebinth known as al Hisha.   The trunks of these trees—and more particularly of the terebinth (*Butm*)—have grown to a goodly girth, often to a diameter of four and five feet, but their foliage, thanks to the attentions of countless generations of goats, is a mere parody of the term.   A few trees happily survive to show what their fellows were like—a trunk of solid timber, three or four feet in diameter at the base and but little less at its top some fifteen or sixteen feet higher, surmounted by a mere bush of scantily-leaved tendrils.   The oaks (*Balut* or *Sindiyan*) are generally less well-grown than the terebinths and, for the most part, form mere thickets whose prickly leaves create the illusion of holly-bushes.   Mistletoe with red berries grows upon them plentifully.   During the War the Turks, being cut off from their ordinary sources of coal-supply, built a railway from Anaiza station to the edge of this forest (Ras al Hadid)—a distance of twenty-two miles—and, sawing off the massive trunks as near the ground as possible, carried them off to burn in the engines of the Hijaz Railway.   This branch-line may some day, if repaired, serve a useful purpose in carrying tourists to Petra, but it will carry them through no forest; the trunkless bases of the old giants, looking from a distance like great slabs of stone scattered about the hillsides, are all that remains with only a few accidental survivors to help one to picture the scene in its former glory.

The southern part of the main range is a bare tract of desert slopes bright with grass and flowers in the spring but dry and parched at other times.   Heavy snows fall during January and February all along the summit of the Shara, and patches of it remain in sheltered nooks and crannies even into

* *Vide* Chapter IV., and Figs. 61 and 62.
† These ruins are fully illustrated and discussed in Brünnow and Domaszewsky, Vol. I., pp. 433 *et seq.*

April.   A good deal of patchy cultivation is carried on, in spots where the soil and gradients are suitable, by the Na'aimat and Liyathina, but the crop has to mature rapidly to escape the parching heat of early summer, and is generally both short in the stalk and light in the ear.

The western slope of the Shara, in contrast with its gently graded eastern ridges, plunges abruptly down in steep slopes and deep valleys, which splendidly exhibit in their lofty cliffs the varied strata of the thick Cretaceous formation, to the Petra level some 2,500 feet below.   The valleys, converging on the two main lines—Wadi Musa and Wadi al Jamal—which form Wadi Musa, abound in springs, about which a good deal of cultivation is attempted, and culminate just above Petra in the extensive terraces of the village of Alji (Fig. 1), in springtime a fragrant mass of fruit blossom, varied by fresh patches of green corn, and standing out with its brilliant lines against the purple background of the Petra crags.

II.—THE APPROACHES TO PETRA

The view of Petra from just above Alji village (Fig. 1), particularly at dawn before the rays of the rising sun have reached the pinnacled summits of the sandstone sierra, is one of infinite, ineffable charm.   The soft hues of the rose-tinted rock-barrier before one will later in the day harden into too crude outlines of light and shadow, but at that hour they float with an appearance of unreality like a veil before the mysteries one has dared to approach.   Few scenes in Nature can more adequately represent that fairyland which is man's dream-picture of perfection.   That scene does, indeed, approach perfection, creating as it does in the beholder a sense of awe and mystery without which the climax of that glimpse of the Khazna temple (Fig. 111)—again before the sun has reached its face or when the moon is upon it—through the darkling walls of the Siq gorge, should not be approached.   It is, indeed, well worth the while of the visitor to arrange the time and manner of his approach to Petra in such a way as to secure the most striking effect upon his senses, but material difficulties of travel—perhaps one should say material facilities now that the motor-car has substantially shortened the journey from the railway—may render this not always feasible.   It so happens, however, that the easiest approach to Petra under modern conditions—it was also the regular approach to it for tourists before the War, though then toilsome and laborious—enjoys the advantage of bringing the visitor with thrilling abruptness to the very verge of the mountain-crest, below which, far below, Petra lies exposed to view in all its glory and, more than Petra, the abyss of the Rift Valley beyond, the summits of distant Midian and the haze-bound uplands of Palestine towards Sinai.   Those who have driven by car from Anaiza station across the plain and along the valley of Ain Najal and up through the treeless forest of al Hisha with the elusive horizon of al Shara ever before them—seemingly impossible to reach as ridge succeeds to ridge—and have come suddenly without warning at Ras al Khaur to the edge of that vast chasm with its tossing sea of ruddy peaks below and have looked down on Petra,* will never forget that scene.   It is one that defies the photographer and cannot be described.

The best—and now the regular—route of approach to Petra is by the track above-mentioned, which at Ain Najal is joined by the former route of " Cook's " tourists from Jerusalem *via* Jericho and across the Dead Sea to Karak and thence *via* Tafila and Shaubak.   Another route, or series of routes, leaves Ma'an in a westerly direction, and runs up to the crest of al Shara, either by Udhra or Basta, or by a track intermediate between them, passing the springs of al Husaiyin.   All these routes reach the crest of the ridge either at Ras al Hatti or a point not far to the southward thereof. Thence rough torrent channels lead down to the head of Wadi al Jamal whose course the track follows

---

* A good idea of this view may be gained from a photograph reproduced in the Frontispiece, taken obliquely from an aeroplane by the officers of the Royal Air Force.

to Alji, which can also be reached *via* the spring of Ain al Hai from Ras al Khaur by those who, arriving there, prefer to enter Petra *via* the Siq rather than to descend straight down the hillside to the Qasr al Bint. From the point already mentioned south of Ras al Hatti several subsidiary tracks follow the crest of the left bank of Wadi al Jamal and either descend into the Bab al Siq area without touching Alji or lead into the latter *via* the spring of Ain al Hah. A branch of the Roman road led from Negla (Ain Najal) to Ras al Khaur through the Hisha forest, where stretches of the old pavement are still to be seen, and thence straight down the hillside to and through the group of monuments known as al Nasara. From here the course of the road through the city is not very clear, but, passing through it, it divided into two branches in the neighbourhood of the " Southern Graves "—one going due south to the outpost of Sabra, and the other south-westward past the south flank of Mount Hor (Jabal Harun) down into the Araba Valley and so to Aqaba. There is also a route from Petra north-westward past the Baidha and Barid tracts into the Araba valley, where it branches out into two tracks, leading respectively to Beersheba and to Jerusalem *via* Hebron. Like all the tracks traversing the region of Nubian sandstone, this route presents much difficulty to mounted parties, being at times steep and rocky, and it is impracticable for camel-transport.

III.—THE CITY AREA

Having thus surveyed in broad outline its immediate surroundings and the channels of approach to it, we may turn our attention to the Petra district itself, which conveniently falls into six well-marked divisions—namely, (1) the city area, comprising the whole basin contained between the two sand-stone folds and the northern and southern watersheds; (2) the main or western ridge, with particular reference to its three outstanding features: Jabal Harun, al Biyara, and the Ma'aisara group; (3) the secondary eastern ridge; (4) the Ramla or Bab al Siq area, with special reference to al Wu'aira and its neighbouring canyons; (5) the northern district, including al Baidha and al Barid; and (6) the southern outpost of Sabra.

The city area (Figs. 5 and 14) is roughly bisected from east to west by the channel of Wadi Musa itself (see Frontispiece), on either side of which the alluvial débris of the surrounding hills, brought down year after year by the seasonal torrents, is piled up in tumbled, undulating masses, whose natural eminences were used by the lords of Petra to form the *points d'appui* of its circuit wall. To north and south, as already noted, this alluvial mass rises from the central line to the Baidha and Sabra watersheds, as they may be called for convenience; and each of these watersheds contributes to the volume of water carried by Wadi Musa through the medium of several channels running down, sometimes in beds of considerable depth, through the soft alluvial soil. Wadi Mataha (Fig. 6), which collects the water of the subsidiary canyons already mentioned at the Sidd al Ma'ajin at the N.E. extremity of the city area, is the first to join Wadi Musa from the north after a short course along the western base of the Khubdha ridge. Next to it westwards is Wadi Nasara (Fig. 6), which descends in the neighbourhood of the Nasara monuments from the Cretaceous slopes behind them, and joins Wadi Musa at the central point of the town area; while, lastly, the eastern flanks of the northern part of the main sandstone ridge are drained by the important channel of Wadi Turkamaniya (Figs. 7 and 8), which converges on Wadi Musa at the top of the Siyagh gorge simultaneously with the three torrent-channels (Fig. 9) of al Ma'aisara—namely, Wadi al Dair, Ma'aisarat al Wasta and Ma'aisarat al Tarfaniya in that order from west to east. On the south side the tributaries of Wadi Musa are Wadi Farasa (Figs. 10 and 11) and its affluents draining the Madhbah area; Wadi Numair draining the hill of that name; Wadi Umm al Ratam further south; and Wadi al Thughra which, draining the southern watershed and the southern portion of the main (western) sandstone ridge, flows along the eastern flank of the latter and, joined by the three channels above-mentioned, coalesces (Fig. 13) with Wadi Musa, or rather the Siyagh, as it has by then become, behind the Habis hill. With a river-system so ample in proportion to the area it covers one might reasonably expect an abundance of subsoil water, but the fact is that throughout the central area perennial water is only to be found at one point in Wadi Turkamaniya, where there is a slender spring and sometimes a rivulet running from it for a few yards. Below the head of the Siyagh, however, there are a series of springs, beginning with Ain al Siyagh about a quarter-mile distant from Qasr al Bint, which give rise to a thin perennial stream flowing down through the gorge. Nevertheless, the *Wadi* channels of the central area are not without vegetation—being thickly covered with oleander bushes, white broom, and other shrubs, whose roots doubtless find sufficient moisture in the sandy soil—while the higher ground is thickly covered with a large bulbous plant resembling the squill. The Petra district has, moreover, quite a special, though limited, animal and insect fauna—the rose-finch occurring here as in Sinai and also the fan-tailed raven, while several new subspecies of butterflies have recently been collected from it. The climate of this area is dry and subtropical with but scanty rainfall and with a temperature rising to 110 F. or more in the summer and seldom falling to anything approaching freezing-point even in the depth of winter. Climatically, therefore, it provides an extraordinary contrast to the lofty, bleak, and often snow-covered ridge of al Shara only a few miles distant, and has, together with the two sandstone ridges (whose summits may frequently experience temperatures below freezing-point, though they do not receive much actual rainfall), greater affinities with the sun-scorched subtropical region of Wadi Araba, Midian, Southern Palestine, and Sinai than with the Arabian desert to the east. As regards elevation the lowest part of the city area—*i.e.*, in the neighbourhood of Qasr al Bint—is approximately 2,773 feet above sea-level, while the mean elevation of the northern and southern watersheds is about 3,350 and 3,250 feet respectively.

IV.—THE WESTERN RANGE

The main or western ridge (Fig. 14), which abruptly separates the Petra district from the Rift Valley of Wadi Araba and its associated limestone foothills, runs for a distance of four or five miles from its highest and most southerly point in Mount Hor to the Baidha ridges on the north. As seen from the east, it forms an unbroken barrier of splendid crags between Petra and the abyss beyond, though, in point of fact, there are several breaches of continuity, deep valleys between the various crag-masses. This mountain barrier is, as already noted, split at right angles to its axis by the deep central canyon of al Siyagh (Figs. 16, 17 and 18). On the left or south of al Siyagh rises the flat-topped boss of Biyara (Fig. 17), between which and the ridge of Barra beyond, a deeply eroded valley, Wadi Barra (Fig. 20), runs down to join the Siyagh. Again between Barra and Mount Hor a similar valley, Wadi al Sutuh, which also eventually joins the Siyagh, makes another break in the apparent continuity of the range. North of the Siyagh rises the splendid mass of peaks and pinnacles forming the Ma'aisara (Fig. 9) block, which in its turn is separated from the low flat ridge forming the southern flank of the Baidha tract by a broad and gently-inclined valley called Abul Ruq'a or Wadi Manatt al Dhib. This channel joins the Siyagh to the westward of the Dair plateau below the mouth of Wadi Marwan. The slopes and ravines of all this area are sparsely clothed with gnarled bushes and even trees of juniper, white-broom, and other vegetation, while Ibex used to be common among the crags before they were exterminated or driven away by the advent of the modern rifle. The summit of Jabal Harun (Mount Hor)—a conspicuous feature of the Petra landscape whencesoever beheld—stands at an elevation of some 4,280 feet above sea-level, while the highest point of the plateau-summit of Biyara has an elevation of 3,609 feet, the Dair plateau (Qasr al Dair) being 3,500 feet in altitude and the highest point of the Barid gorge about 100 feet lower. The mean elevation of the whole range may be taken, therefore, as being approximately 3,600 or 3,700 feet above sea-level, to which it drops with extraordinary abruptness on the Wadi Araba side—the actual level of the latter at this point being only some 700 feet above sea-level. This whole range is of dark ruddy sandstone except in the Baidha area, where the hummocks and knolls into which the sandstone has weathered are of a dazzling whiteness and belong geologically to the eastern ridge rather than that of which they constitute a geographical continuation. Mention has already been made of a thin wedge of porphyritic rocks (Fig. 2), which runs north and south for a distance of two miles through the western portion of the range from a point opposite Jabal Harun to a point immediately north of the Siyagh gorge, which cuts through it.

Jabal Harun (see Figs. 1 and 20 and Plate II.), the highest of the Petra peaks, has been identified by some authorities as Mount Hor and, according to Muslim and local tradition, claims the honour of bearing on its summit the tomb of Aaron (Fig. 21), from which it takes its Arabic name. Muslim fanaticism for this reason has always placed obstacles in the way of visitations to the mountain by other than Muslim pilgrims, for whom Fridays are the most suitable days of pilgrimage—in fact, it is only on those days that the custodian, a resident of Alji, betakes himself to the tomb for the purpose of admitting visitors to the interior. Fridays should accordingly be avoided by the non-Muslim visitor, for whom the tomb has no intrinsic interest, while the view to be enjoyed from its summit well repays the considerable labour of the ascent. The guides must, of course, be squared by the promise of silence and something more solid before they will consent to take an infidel up. The track from Qasr al Bint leads southwards up Wadi Thughra (Fig. 15), from whose watershed beyond the " Southern Graves " it drops into the channel of Wadi al Sutuh, and follows it to the base of the mountain. The ascent over the rough stony slope at first presents no difficulty, but as the summit is approached the path becomes progressively steeper, narrower, and more difficult, while the most difficult parts have been made possible by steps cut into the rock. The whole of the ascent can be made on ponies up to a broad plateau immediately below the lofty knoll on whose summit the tomb is perched (Fig. 12). Here, amid some ruins of massive masonry, one dismounts to ascend a narrow and steep gully (Fig. 22), whose lower extremity is blocked by a masonry barrel-roofed reservoir supported by fifteen Roman arches and still capable of holding water, the walls being covered over with cement. A climb of fifteen minutes, in some places up a stepped path and in others by slabs of rock placed in convenient positions, leads up to a platform on the summit on which stands the shrine—a white-washed domed building (Fig. 21) of rough masonry partly covered with plaster. It measures $37\frac{1}{2}$ feet from north to south and $32\frac{1}{2}$ feet from east to west, and the dome stands over the north-east corner of the roof, whose corners are adorned with fragments of Roman marble. An Arabic inscription over the doorway on the south side gives the date of the construction of the building as A.H. 900 (the last figure is, however, scarcely legible, and it may be anything from 900 to 909)=A.D. 1495 approximately. The cracks of the wooden door allow one a glimpse of the interior—a chamber containing a stone sarcophagus with a canopy over its lid. The view from the summit is magnificent, especially towards the north, where the whole of Petra and Wadi Araba lie before one, spread out as a map, with the line of Wadi Musa flowing into the latter far below, while the great temple of the Dair plateau stands out visibly (Fig. 23) from its setting of crags. On a clear day the south end of the Dead Sea should be easily visible over the porphyritic ridge already mentioned, while the southern

c

horizon is closed in by the mountains of Midian. The return journey can be materially shortened by a rough scramble down the east face of the mountain, by which a very rough path leads down to the Thughra watershed.

Diodorus Siculus* mentions that the Nabataeans were in the habit of attending a great fair at some place not named and of leaving during their absence " their possessions and their oldest men along with their wives and children " in a rock which was a place of great strength, " though without walls and distant from the inhabited part a two-days' journey." It may be that he was merely referring vaguely—and somewhat inaccurately—to† Petra generally, but it may be suggested that he was, in fact, speaking with extraordinary accuracy of detail of a particular locality in the Petra district—namely, the conspicuous flat-topped mountain now known as al Biyara (Fig. 24), which is the outstanding feature of the main sandstone range northward of Jabal Harun. At any rate, the details he gives of " the rock " in another passage—namely, that there was " only one way up, made by hand "—exactly fit this locality, which also provides a striking illustration of the Nabataean practice of building cisterns for the storage of water—" great caves, the mouths of which they make quite small, but, ever increasing the width of them deep down, they at last render the size so great that each side measures a plethrum." The cisterns on the summit of al Biyara are the only ones known in the sandstone area—*i.e.*, Petra proper—which exactly fit that description.

Be that as it may, the summit of al Biyara consists of a plateau of considerable dimensions, sloping gently from its‡ highest point at the north-western corner in an easterly or south-easterly direction. The mountain mass falls on the northern, western, and eastern sides in steep precipices which would appear to be practically inaccessible, while the only way up starts at the south-eastern corner and climbs the rough crags constituting the southern flank or rather buttress. At, or near, the bottom of the ascent this way enters a narrow gully, which still shows the ruins of a masonry gateway, obviously built at some time as a defensive measure. At some little distance further up the gully ends in a double couloir (Fig. 31), obviously artificial, and leading up to right and left respectively on to a bluff, from which a made stairway, numerous sections of which are still to be seen at intervals, leads from crag to crag up to the summit. The plateau-summit consists of bare rock towards the west and north-west, but its sloping surface is elsewhere well covered with soil on which grows a profusion of desert sage (*Shih*), as well as stunted junipers, white broom, and other bushes. There is plenty of room here for the sojourn of a considerable multitude, which would find all the water it required in a group of four cisterns of the kind referred to by Diodorus, well cemented internally and actually containing water in the spring of 1924. Their mouths are about two feet in diameter, and they occupy the lowest edge of the plateau (about 120 feet lower than the highest north-western point), so that they would catch the drainage of its whole surface. Here and there the rim of the plateau bears clear traces of a very rough and primitive wall made of uncut slabs of loose rock.

The conspicuous mass of this mountain is isolated from the rest of the range of which it forms part by the deep valleys of Wadi Barra and al Siyagh, which meet from the south-east and east respectively at its western corner. The view down this gorge (Fig. 26) from the summit of al Biyara is extremely imposing, and the same view-point affords the best obtainable panorama of Petra as a whole. Southward the summits of Jabal Harun and Barra stand out the most conspicuous features of a splendid ridge, while south-eastward (Fig. 25) one looks out over the southern watershed to the head of the Sabra valley and the ridge of al Shara beyond. The best view of al Biyara itself is, perhaps, to be

---

* *Vide* Chapter III.   † The word actually used for " Rock " is πετρα.
‡ Approximately 3,732 feet above sea-level—*i.e.*, 959 feet above the city area.

obtained looking south-west (Fig. 24) from the left bank of Wadi Turkamaniya over the inconspicuous lump of al Habis, from which it is separated by Wadi Thughra just before its confluence with al Siyagh. This view, showing the east and north faces of the mountain, gives a good idea of the extent of the plateau on the summit. The north-eastern corner of the mountain is distinguished by a well-marked natural platform (Fig. 29) about one-third of the way up and overlooking Wadi Thughra, but, apart from the existence of a large cave in the rock face, this feature does not show any sign of having ever been utilised in any way by the human occupants of Petra; there would certainly seem to be no feasible track leading from it to the summit.

The deep gorge of al Siyagh divides the Biyara mountain from al Ma'aisara, which may justly be given pride of place as the finest group of crags and ravines in the Western range and, indeed, in the whole of the Petra district. The gorge, so far as we were able to ascertain, does not afford a practicable route from Petra to Wadi Araba. A thick growth of oleanders and other shrubs completely blocks the bed of the torrent at a point just below Ain al Siyagh, whence a goat-track leads up round the flank of the Dair hill. From this track, which rapidly rises to a considerable height above the steeply descending stream-bed, the course of the latter can be seen striking through the saw-like arête of the porphyritic ridge (Fig. 2) and meandering in a maze of tumbled folds beyond it to the flank of Jabal Atud (Frontispiece), whence it is said to plunge down abruptly in a cascade into the area of the foothills on the border of Wadi Araba. The porphyritic ridge appears to come to an end on the western flank of the Dair hill at the junction of Wadi Marwan with al Siyagh. A rough climb from its summit brings one up on to a sandstone slope, which rises to the western edge of the Dair plateau, whence is to be obtained a splendid view (Fig. 20) of Jabal Harun and the rest of the mountain system to the southward. The view to the north is cut off by the inaccessible summits of the Dair crags, which themselves form part of the Ma'aisara group (Fig. 9), occupying the whole area bounded by Wadi Turkamaniya on the east, the Siyagh-Marwan junction on the west, the Siyagh gorge on the south, and the valley of Manatt al Dhib on the north. This great massif of dark ruddy sandstone rises to a height of some 1,200 to 1,500 feet above the town area in a galaxy of pinnacles and bosses, and is scored in every direction by steep valleys and abrupt ravines and gullies. The southernmost summit (Fig. 16), forming the southern bastion of the Dair plateau and overlooking al Siyagh, bears the name of Taraf al Dair. It is parted eastward from the great buttress of the Dair hill itself (Fig. 19) by the deep gully of what is called by Dr. Dalman the *Klausenschlucht* and by the Arabs Wadi Taraf al Dair (Fig. 27). The Dair hill is continued north-eastward by a jagged ridge, whose flank is scored by two minor gullies, and which ends in the summit of Hadhbat al Zaitun (Fig. 19 in centre). On the right (north-east) of the latter the Ma'aisara group is cleft by the valley of Wadi al Dair* (Fig. 9), whose upper reaches are fed by numerous gullies. The most important of these, and the one which gives its name to the whole valley, is that descending from the eastern edge of the Dair plateau, where is also the head of the *Klausenschlucht*. Halfway down this ravine is joined from the north by a gully of no great length known as al Qattar (Fig. 28), at whose head is a bower-like grotto adorned with ferns and mosses and partly covered over by a natural arch of the overhanging sandstone through which water trickles down the side walls from an unknown source. Still further down the main ravine is joined at right angles from the north by a nameless affluent whose narrow bed completely severs the crags of the Dair group from those of al Ma'aisara properly so called. At this point, immediately above the "Lion tomb," the Wadi turns sharply southwards and presents a charming view (Fig. 30) between the walls of its narrow gorge over the Petra area to Mount Seir beyond from the crest of a transverse precipice of some height, over which the stream

---

* Brünnow's "first N.W. Wadi," called "Wadi al Dair" by Dalman.

must pour in flood time to the sandy valley below. This obstacle is negotiated by human traffic (pilgrims in the past and tourists in our own time) by way of a rock-cut couloir which has itself been partially blocked up by an enormous boulder fallen from above (Fig. 32). Wadi al Dair is joined shortly below this fall by the central valley of the Ma'aisara group, which is known as Wadi Ma'aisarat al Wastani* (Fig. 33), and arrives at the lower level over a narrow fall. The combined Wadi is joined at the head of al Siyagh by the channels of Wadi Ma'aisarat al Tarfani,† which cleaves the eastern section of the Ma'aisara group, and Wadi Turkamaniya.‡ The three Wadis of the Ma'aisara system are clearly seen in Fig. 9. The central block of crags between the two more easterly valleys would seem to be the loftiest of the system, comprising two summits, of which the one towards the west is the higher and bears almost due north from Qasr al Bint. The easterly block of the Ma'aisara mass (Fig. 19 on right), lying between Wadi Ma'aisarat al Tarfani and Wadi Turkamaniya, is known as " Udhrat al Hisha," and also consists of two peaks.

V.—THE EASTERN RANGE

The eastern or secondary sandstone ridge differs from the main range in being less elevated and in its northern sections of a more uniform appearance without outstanding pinnacles and summits (Fig. 34 shows the crags of the Dair hill in the foreground and the white ridge of al Khubdha beyond). It is largely composed, particularly in its northern and eastern portions, of the same dazzling-white sandstone (Fig. 35), which has been noted in reference to the Baidha tract, which is geologically a continuation of it. The ruddy sandstone, which occupies its western face and southern portions, is also of a more varied colouring than that of the western range, being here and there " shot " with all the colours of the rainbow, of which the ancient settlers of Petra took advantage in the excavation of their tombs and other monuments. The northern extremity of the ridge is deflected westward from the head of Wadi Mataha to the head of Wadi Turkamaniya in the neighbourhood of al Najr and thus includes the Nasara tract (Fig. 6) and in effect forms the northern watershed of the city area, while from Wadi Mataha its main line runs (Fig. 5) southward with a mean elevation of some 3,350 feet through al Khubdha and the Obelisk ridge to Jabal Numair, beyond which it is continued in the two ridges of ruddy sandstone which forms the flanks of Wadi Sabra (Fig. 58).

The great domed summit of al Khubdha (Fig. 36), rising above a curiously regular mass of lower domes, all of white sandstone and parted from each other by garden-plots, as it were, and grassy lawns, stands at an elevation of approximately 3,608 feet above sea-level, and the summit of Numair (Fig. 11) would seem to be of similar height. The dome-like configuration of the white sandstone area contrasts markedly with the flattened summits of the red sandstone, which forms a narrow elongated plateau, through which the gorge of the Siq carves its deep and winding path. The western face of this ridge (Fig. 36) fronts the Petra basin in a sheer precipice, interrupted at intervals by headlong ravines, of which that known as Naqb al Khubdha al Gharbi is a good example, as also are the gullies descending to the Khazna from both sides, the ravine of Wadi Mahafir descending from the Obelisk ridge to the theatre and the many abrupt glens giving birth to the Farasa Wadis (Figs. 10 and 11). More gentle gradients are found on the eastern versant, where the plateau can be approached without difficulty by way of the tract called al Madras to the south of the Siq, though north of the gorge the approach to the Khubdha heights from the east is as precipitous and fearful as by any of the

---

* Brünnow's " second N.W. Wadi," called " Ma'aisarat al Tarfani " by Dalman.
† Brünnow's " third N.W. Wadi," called " Ma'aisarat al Wasta " by Dalman.
‡ Called by Dalman " Wadi abu Olleka " and " Wadi el Hise."

western ravines.   Indeed, the only really practicable route on this side is by what is known as Naqb al Khubdha al Sharqi, which finally drops (and much agility is needed in negotiating it) into Wadi Mudhlim over a 20-foot precipice.   Another ravine in this area which deserves a passing notice is that of Wadi Huraimiya (Fig. 37), which descends from al Madras into the Siq itself, but becomes absolutely impracticable about halfway down owing to a series of steep falls.

There were noticed on the air-plane survey made in 1923—in a position somewhere north of the Turkamaniya tomb—outlines which clearly indicated the existence of monuments or of walls prepared for them.   Examination on the spot showed the existence of the notable rockwork of Fig. 39 on the top of a ridge (Fig. 40) nearly closing up the Turkamaniya Wadi a mile north of the tomb, a little to the left (west) of the route to Ras al Khaur.   Fig. 39 shows the southern of the two main masses which compose this feature, whose name was said by the Arabs to be al Najr, a name which has been also given to a hill between the Obelisk ridge and Jabal Numair.*

The huge, squared faces are from 40 to 50 feet in height.   The object of spending so much labour on them must have been either simply for quarrying or else by way of preparation for the carving of future monuments which were never completed.   Neither the place nor the method seems quite consistent with the former supposition, so that their actual origin must remain undecided. These masses consist of red sandstone, but they are on the western edge of the huge mass of white sandstone which crosses the main valley north of Nasara.   On the top of the southern block we found all the signs of use as a place of cult.   The southern block of al Najr sags in the middle to a craggy gap or depression lying roughly east and west.   A track, consisting here and there of steps cut in the rock, ascends by this gap from the ground-level to the summit, near which a perilous path leads round the lip of the precipitous eastern flank of the block on to a contoured slope facing northwards (see Fig. 39) and having all the appearance of having been intended to provide seating accommodation for the spectators whom we may suppose to have attended the ceremonies enacted in this " high place."   Below these tiers of seats the northern faces of the block fall in a sheer (artificial) precipice, at the top of which in a central position the rock is cut out in blocks and runnels—possibly an altar; though, if the theory be accepted that the whole mass formed a quarry, it may be that we see in these blocks separated by grooves the actual process of quarrying in arrested action.   The western extremity of the steps ends in a two-sided level court, open to north and east, bounded by a plain rock-face on the south, and having on the west side a sort of shrine, consisting of a low wall decorated with two blank " omphali," and surmounted by a step or platform leading to a triple idol or altar composed of three flat or slightly convex blocks.   At the back (west) of this shrine in another court is what would appear to be the main idol—a triple block (Fig. 41) like the previous one, but of much greater size.   This idol-group lies near the northern extremity of the court, whose eastern side is occupied by the other, while on the south it is bounded by a plain wall, whose only decoration is a minute recessed niche only 12 inches high by 6 inches broad.   The west wall of the court is partly plain, and partly contoured (as shown in Figs. 41 and 42), the centre of the contoured portion being adorned with another triple-block idol (to the right of the seated figure in Fig. 42) backed by a wide flat platform.   A water-runnel along the base of the west wall terminates in the main idol through which it would seem to have drained the court and its surroundings.   In Fig. 39 the main idol is seen just to the right of a conspicuous bush, with the west wall of the court behind it somewhat to the right; the crags in the background belong not to the Najr block, as one might think from the photograph, but to the ridge separated from it by the Wadi Turkamaniya.   Fig. 42 shows the main idol again

---

* The northern face of this hill has, like the face of the Najr block, been smoothed as if for a façade. It is shown in Fig. 209.

(in front of the standing figure) with the west wall behind it. The northern block of al Najr, and a considerable tract beyond it northwards, below, and west of the road to Ras al Khaur, contain innumerable evidences of cult significance, specimens of which are shown in Figs. 43 and 44. Still further north the Ras al Khaur road runs through another group of cult monuments at the edge of a tributary of Wadi Turkamaniya called Umm Saihun, a part of whose " high place " is shown in the foreground of Fig. 45, with the crags of the Turkamaniya watershed behind it. It will be noted that the white sandstone here crosses the northern extremity of the Petra depression from east to west, the rocks on the left of the photograph being of the ruddy sandstone and belonging to the Ma'aisara ridge. In the white rocks is a group of monumental tombs (Fig. 47), one of which is particularly striking. The Ras al Khaur road passes over the white sandstone close to and immediately behind this monument—in fact, practically over its roof.

VI.—AL RAMLA

The Ramla or Bab al Siq area forms an easy transition from the Cretaceous ridge to the sandstone folds. Composed of white sandstone, rounded into dome-like shapes like the Khubdha, it is separated in its northern part (the Wu'aira tract), from the Cretaceous slope behind it by a deep and narrow cleft, while further south its separation from the exposed sandstone strata underlying the limestones of the main ridge (Al Shara) is almost imperceptible. Through it centrally from east to west runs the channel and valley of Wadi Musa, while its northern section is cut north and south into slices by the deep subsidiary canyons to which reference has been made. Remnants of a Cretaceous covering are still to be observed here and there on the summits of this tract, from which it may be inferred that, having formerly been under the extreme edge of the Cretaceous sea, it was thrown forward by the movements which created the Rift Valley and has since been almost entirely denuded of its original thin Cretaceous stratum by normal weathering. The village of Alji (Fig. 1) and the streams which water its orchards and fields belong rather to the Cretaceous area than to Ramla, but the latter tract for the greater part of the year enjoys the advantage of a running stream, whose extent westward is determined from season to season by the amount of rainfall and the demands of the Alji cultivators. The Wadi bed and banks are thickly covered with oleander bushes, and the valley, almost marshy in parts, provides luscious grazing for the few kine of the village and for its horses and mules. An ancient reservoir known as al Birka (Fig. 46) stands at some distance back from the right bank of the valley at its entrance into the Ramla tract, its walls being partly of " Cyclopean " masonry and partly the natural rock which abuts on its northern side. And there is reason to believe that this tank was used on occasion to replenish the water-supply of the city through the medium of an elaborate system of aqueducts running northwards through the main north-south canyon of Sha'ib al Qais (Fig. 48). The channels are for the most part cut out of the rock-walls of the valley, but where necessary they were carried across the openings of side ravines on masonry arches, one of which still survives at the northern end of Sha'ib al Qais, and is locally known as al Qantara (Fig. 188). The Sha'ib al Qais, in addition to carrying this aqueduct, appears to have been an important highway, if we may judge by the frequent occurrence in its course—and particularly about midway down it, near a large block of rock fallen from the hillside above—of emblems and appurtenances of cult. One of these deserve special mention—namely, a very well-marked stibadium (Fig. 49) in an excellent state of preservation; it is, of course, carved out in the living rock, and a roadway, clearly artificial, runs past it.

The most westerly of the Ramla canyons, all of which converge on the head of Wadi Mataha and the gully of Sidd al Ma'ajin, is Wadi al Mudhlim, which, diverted through the (apparently) natural tunnel of al Mudhlim from the head of the Siq, bifurcates further down. The direct continuation of the Wadi Mudhlim channel was found to be impracticable, but the easterly fork, called Maqaris al Sulaib, provides an easy route down to its junction with the lower reaches of Sha'ib al Qais, which may be regarded as the principal canyon. This valley is practicable from its tail to its head in the domed rocks near al Birka, from the neighbourhood of which a side valley leads up by a difficult track to the castle of al Wu'aira (see p. 36), which occupies a considerable area on a group of domed white sandstone summits (Fig. 50) between the valley of Sha'ib al Qais to the east and the narrow cleft which separates it on the west from the slope of al Shara. Here there are numerous ruins of masonry buildings with rounded arches, and of barrel-vaulted chambers, which have been described in detail by Professor Alois Musil. The most interesting of these ruins is the remains of what may be a basilica or Crusader church with the apsed extremity still standing. A line of low battlemented and loopholed wall runs along the eastern edge of this fortress overlooking the cleft already mentioned and facing the great slope of al Shara beyond it. It was only on that side that an enemy could effectively attack the position, owing to the fact that the Shara slope completely dominates the Wu'aira summit.

VII.—AL BAIDHA AND AL BARID

The Baidha tract (Fig. 51) on the north lies in relation to the Ras al Khaur ridge and the sandstone folds very much as the Ramla tract does between the Ras al Hatti ridge and the Khubdha tract—forming geologically a transition-stage between two epochs, strategically and politically an outpost, and commercially a gateway or suburb to Petra. As the Ramla tract formed the approach to the ceremonial entrance of the city, so the Baidha suburb, athwart the only road leading to the principal marts of Palestine, bears abundant signs of having been a position of great importance. Here was undoubtedly the halting-place of all caravans from Palestine and the starting-point for all going thither. Sepulchral monuments and temples are here to be found, it is true, but they are few in number compared with the warehouses and offices of merchants and the numerous reservoirs for the storage of water. Baidha was, we may safely assume, the commercial quarter of Petra.

Geographically speaking, the Baidha ridge may be regarded either as cutting off the main Petra range on the north or as forming a northward continuation of it. Between the massif of Ma'aisara, the northern extremity of the main range, and the Baidha ridge (Fig. 52), which runs roughly in an east and west direction, lies a wide valley or plain with a slope towards the southwest. It is traversed by the bed of Wadi Manatt al Dhib descending from the Cretaceous ridge on the east and joined in mid-course by the valley of Abu Ruq'a, which cleaves through the Baidha ridge from a northerly direction.

The normal approach from Petra is by a route following the course of Wadi Turkamaniya (Figs. 7 and 8) upwards to its watershed, and thence descending with an easy gradient through the scattered tumuli of white sandstone to a wide open space (Fig. 51), which appears to have served as a camping ground for caravans. Another route ascends the middle channel (Fig. 33) of Ma'aisara (Ma'aisarat al Wasta) to the west of Wadi Turkamaniya and, crossing Wadi Manatt al Dhib, follows the course of Wadi Abu Ruq'a through the Baidha ridge to some ruins which appear to have formed a fort commanding the approach from this side. Along the latter and more direct track frequent traces still survive of a road, 6 to 8 feet in width, cut out of the rock to facilitate communication between city and suburb, while the spiritual welfare of people using it appears to have been amply provided for. A wide bulge of the Ma'aisarat al Wasta valley near its watershed contains extensive remnants of masonry foundations, betokening the existence here of a fort or caravanserai for the protection or convenience of travellers. A small tank stands under a perpendicular cliff on its west side, and the rock walls on either side contain numerous idol-niches and shrines, while close by the road lies a somewhat rough and primitive " High Place." A hummock of rock at some distance to the west of the road in the Wadi Manatt al Dhib valley is surmounted by masonry ruins which may have been a watch-tower or guard-post.

The first monument of the Baidha area proper on this track stands at the exit of Wadi Abu Ruq'a from the Baidha ridge on a low excrescence of rock at some distance to the east of its bed. It is a tomb excavated out of the rock at a height of 20 feet above ground-level and approached by a flight of steps; its façade, so weathered that no trace of its original design can be made out, stands out about one foot from the flattened rock-face and is pierced with a doorway 4 feet high and 2½ feet wide, leading into a chamber (6×4×6 feet), whose floor shelves roughly down to a grave-cavity about 2 feet deep. This monument is of interest rather from its position on a detached block of rock at the very entrance to the Baidha area on this side than for any architectural reason.

Beyond it on the left bank of the Wadi is an unimportant " High Place " with a crescent-shaped recess, a depression for holding water and other customary accessories, while the rock lining the opposite bank is curiously contoured into steps with slender water-runnels between them, the purpose of which it is difficult to fathom. On the left bank further on is an open court or recess of the " fives-court " type, with side walls sloping down to ground-level from the back wall, and containing shallow round-arched recesses on either side. Beyond this, on the same side, is a plain chamber, with slightly arched doorway, and close by in a detached hummock is a larger chamber (9×9×3 feet) with a row of small crowsteps—those at either end half crowsteps only—on a plain architrave above a plain doorway. A runnel, beginning in a cranny in the neighbouring rockside and crossing the intervening ground, runs round the side of the hummock to the edge of the doorway, but no reservoir or receptacle to hold water is in evidence, and it may be that the chamber itself—the doorway having been subsequently cut—may have been originally a reservoir, a conclusion which the lowness of its ceiling would seem to support.

A few open caves of no interest are to be seen in the upper part of the Abu Ruq'a valley, which is shut in at a wide bulge by a masonry dyke, over one end of which rises an earth-covered pile of ruins which appear to have been a fort. A considerable area in this neighbourhood is strewn with scattered remnants of masonry, while not far distant up the valley is what appears to have been a " High Place " (Fig. 53) of considerable importance. It occupies a large flat-topped rock isolated in the midst of the valley, and is arranged as follows: (*a*) An open court, 25×20 feet, on the ground-level at the north-east extremity, with plain back wall and slanting sides; (*b*) on the left side of this court a stibadium carved out of a domed block of rock, whose summit holds a circular depression for water about 2 feet across—a similar waterhole lying close by on the flat summit of another branch of the main rock; (*c*) the upper part of the back-wall of the open court is contoured at the top and contains two oblong niches, while the right-hand wall has a small arched niche scooped out of it; (*d*) a flight of steps leads up between this court and the stibadium to the flat summit of the main rock, in which is a small rectangular tank and whose north edge is cut out to form a ledge; (*e*) in the middle of the platform rises an excrescence of rock on which is an open court (shown in Fig. 53) with back-wall and sloping sides adorned with shallow round-arched recesses and rectangular niches; and (*f*) at the south-west extremity of the main rock are several irregular excrescences which have been cut to form seats or benches. About 75 feet to the north of (*a*) is a rectangular reservoir, consisting of three sections, the largest (9×9×3 feet) being sloped from west to east, and connecting by a hole in its eastern flank with the next, a smaller tank (3×3×3 feet), which, being similarly sloped, connects by a hole with an inclined shute with runnels on either side, whose purpose was apparently to carry off the water issuing from the tanks on to the plain. Traces of roads cut through rocky outcrops in this neighbourhood also appear to be in some way connected with the purposes of the " High Place," while at a short distance east of the reservoir is a triple rock-hewn chamber, consisting of (1) a plain rectangular hall (9×9×15 feet), entered through a plain doorway with empty lintel-sockets and window above the lintel; (2) a rectangular chamber with arched roof (8 feet long and 7 feet broad) and three sepulchral cavities grooved for lids; and (3) a single grave cavity (3×3 feet at its opening, but 3×6×6 feet within) recessed into the back-wall of (b) at a level of 2 feet above the graves therein.

The valley now debouches into the Baidha area (Fig. 51) proper—a scattered mass of white tumuli and rock-masses, many of which contain burial chambers (one of these is shown in Fig. 54), courts, reservoirs, niches, etc., in a considerable plain, an arm of which runs up in a northerly direction into a rock-girt bay, following whose edge one comes suddenly upon the entrance to the Siq al Barid. This is a narrow gorge, cleaving the ridge from north-east to south-west, which, owing to its easily defensible character, was selected by the ancients as the principal business street of the suburb. In front of the entrance on the right-hand side stands a neat and apparently unfinished tomb of classical style (Fig. 38), approached by a flight of low steps, and consisting of a façade flanked by pilasters surmounted by Nabataean capitals and supporting a frieze of four medallions, over which rises a curved arch with stands for urns at each side and over the centre. The interior consists of a plain chamber, 10 feet long, 6 feet broad, and 15 feet high, entered by a doorway of the same dimensions as regards width and height, on either side of which stand pilasters with Nabataean capitals supporting a plain pediment with an urn at its apex.

The entrance to the Barid gorge (Fig. 55) is blocked by a great mass of rock through which a narrow passage, only a few feet in width and about 115 feet long, has been cut, though it may be that the passage is a natural crack developed by human agency, as the artificially smoothed faces of the rock-wall on either side seem to indicate. Sockets at the outer extremity of this passage show that it was formerly fitted with a door or gate, while at the other end the wall has been scooped out to make a platform presumably for the convenience of the guard posted there to prevent unauthorised intrusion. From this point the gorge widens out into a street, whose lofty rock-walls on either side exhibit an elegant array of ornamented and plain façades—temples, offices, residences, warehouses, and reservoirs. These chambers, space being limited, have been excavated, in two and frequently three storeys, one above the other, and the whole area is sprinkled with rock-carved staircases—in many cases destroyed or partly destroyed by the ravages of time—giving access to the higher monuments. The whole of the chambers of the lowest storeys, or at least those which are sunk to a considerable depth below ground-level, forming basements and semi-basements, appear to have served as reservoirs for the storage of water, the collection of which from the crags towering above the gorge was ingeniously provided for by an elaborate arrangement of runnels, aqueducts, and shutes connecting the natural catchment-basins in the hillsides with the interior of the subterranean tanks.

Above a collection of such tanks on the left-hand side of the gorge close to the entrance rises a temple building (Fig. 56) which, in simplicity of line and beauty, ranks high among the monuments of Petra. The façade consists of two perpendicular pilasters, with Nabataean capitals supporting a plain double architrave, whose central weight is borne by two pillars carved in the round and topped with similar capitals. Further on an elaborate " High Place " (Fig. 57) occupies the ledges of a projection of rock which forms an island, or rather peninsula, and restricts the street to narrower proportions. Not far beyond these on the right-hand side of the street and flush with the ground-level stands a group of three large chambers, whose façades are adorned by perpendicular pilasters

D

with plain bevelled capitals.   The pilasters of the third or most southerly chamber are badly damaged, while in all three cases the interiors are quite plain except in the case of the middle chamber, whose back-wall carries an arched recess with two sockets—perhaps to hold idols or candelabra—in its base. These chambers may, perhaps, have served as shops, as also another chamber with similar façade and a rectangular recess (with what appears to be the base of an idol) in its back-wall on the opposite side of the street.   On the same side as this last chamber steps lead up to a " High Place " with a tank (10×3 feet), water-runnels, a niche, and a loculus containing what appears to be a diminutive idol.

A little further on, on the same side, we come to what is one of the most attractive monuments of Petra—a biclinium approached by a stairway, and consisting of a rectangular chamber open towards the gorge with an arched recess or alcove at the back.   The walls of the main chamber, on either side of this alcove are covered with stucco picked out in ochreous paint to give it the appearance of masonry, while its floor is raised two feet above the floor of the hall, which is entered by a broad doorway. The floor of the alcove is raised six inches above the level of that of the chamber, and its arched roof is covered with stucco delicately painted* with a scene of revelry whose details are somewhat difficult to make out in the present damaged state of the ceiling, but appear to be as follows: (1) The whole of the design on the back half of the ceiling is irretrievably lost; (2) the scene depicted on the left-hand front quartering appears to represent Orpheus (or, perhaps, a woman) in a state of nudity, seated with his hair flowing down his back, and playing on a pipe or some such instrument; below and with his back turned to him is a winged Cupid drawing a bow; and the scene, a bower of entangled vines and creepers with a flower resembling the convolvulus, is filled in with another winged Cupid leaping or dancing, a black and white bird and a human hand belonging to a figure which has disappeared; and (3) the scene on the right-hand front quartering is a bower of vines, with bunches of grapes depending from leafy stalks, in the midst of which are three birds and a nude female figure whose face and breasts are visible above and below her arms stretched out towards a bunch of grapes. The central point of the ceiling is marked by a circular medallion with incised markings.

Nearly opposite this biclinium and at about the same level is a " High Place," with tank, aqueducts and seats forming an open-air biclinium.   And at no great distance in a south-westerly direction the Siq gorge comes to an end—its whole length being about a quarter mile—with a long and steep flight of steps between the high and precipitous flanks of a narrow ravine.   A block of fallen rock almost completely obstructs the passage, leaving a space of a few inches only, beyond which the steps continue to a point, whence, through a short descending ravine, one looks out south and west over a splendid wilderness of rock and crag.

The only monument of the Baidha area, in the neighbourhood of the Barid Siq, which calls for a special notice is an enormous reservoir in the white rock-face looking eastward towards Ras al Khaur over an outlying mass of small ridges and hummocks, in which are a few chambers and traces of high places and tanks.   The reservoir within the rock-face is 40 feet long (north and south) and 30 feet wide and about 40 feet deep, its bottom being at the ground-level of the cliff.   The wall-face of the cliff forms the front of the cavity to a height of 20 feet, and the actual eastward opening of the reservoir at that level is approached by a dangerous flight of steps cut into the side of the rock on the south side.   The interior of the reservoir, whose bottom is reached by a flight of steps descending into it on the south side, contains two partition walls reaching about half-way across, and probably left at the time of excavation as supports to the roof.   A broad, deep aqueduct leads from the hillside above to the top of the reservoir, and appears to have been its only source of supply.

* Père Abel gave a photograph of this ceiling in Vol. III. of the *Revue Biblique* (new series), p. 582, etc.

VIII.—WADI SABRA

The southern extremity of the Petra district is the Sabra valley (Fig. 58), which runs down from the southern side of the south watershed between two outlying parallel ridges of sandstone until, meeting a projection of the Cretaceous ridge, it is diverted to the west and runs down into Wadi Araba round the southern flank of Mount Hor. The only importance of this valley, which is of some width, is that it has a perennial spring and rivulet about a mile below the watershed, and it was for that reason occupied in Roman times by a military outpost for the defence of Petra against attack from the south. Close by the spring there is a mass of tumbled masonry, with occasional broken pillars and capitals marking the site of the barracks and other buildings of the Roman garrison, while the mouth of a ravine issuing from the hillside on the left bank of the Wadi was ingeniously made by the garrison to serve the purposes of a theatre (Fig. 59)—its seats being carved out of the sloping sandstone rock-face, while the bed of the ravine itself, intervening between the two wings of the theatre, was bridged by masonry seats built over a drain designed to carry off the water descending the ravine into the main Wadi. The Sabra outpost lies at an elevation of about 2,540 feet above sea-level, and is thus the lowest of the Petra localities. An abundant supply of excellent water and the amenities of the theatre doubtless attracted a small colony of merchants in addition to the garrison of the place, and we may conjecture that the locality also served as a winter-resort for inhabitants of the capital desiring a change of air or a holiday. The bed of the valley downstream of the spring is spread over with a thick covering of luxuriant vegetation (Fig. 60), through which the (apparently) perennial stream runs for a considerable distance. The containing ridges of Wadi Sabra constitute, as has been suggested above, a natural continuation of the ruddy sandstone strata of the eastern ridge, which runs down from the north to Jabal Manza (Fig. 58) at the head of the valley and thence bifurcates.

Finally, in connection with the Wadi Sabra, it should be mentioned that the Air survey of Petra has disclosed the existence of a second broad valley (Plate III.), apparently descending from south-west to north-east through the sandstone block lining the east or left bank of the Wadi. From its position and general appearance it would seem likely that it is traversed by a practicable route and, therefore, needed guarding against an enemy. If this is so, it is not unlikely that it may contain monuments, cult-emblems and other features of interest, to say nothing of a fort. Unfortunately we did not suspect the existence of any such valley—and our guides never volunteered any information about it—until it was too late. It can only be suggested, therefore, that it remains for an enterprising traveller of the future to probe a secret which we failed to explore and the discovery of which, like the discovery of the " High Place " on al Najr, stands to the credit of the Royal Air Force.

CHAPTER II

BIBLIOGRAPHY

THE bibliography of Petra is much more notable for its quantity than for its quality and, with the exception, in fact, of three investigators, or parties of investigators who published their results early in the present century, there is next to nothing which has any scientific value in the older accounts.

Within modern times attention was first drawn to Petra by John Lewis Burckhardt. This gentleman was a young Swiss who had been sent to Aleppo to study and acquire the manners and customs of Moslems by an "Association for Promoting the Discovery of the Interior Parts of Africa." He made himself entirely familiar with Arabic, and was able by dress and speech to pass generally for an Oriental.

It appears that Seetzen, an earlier traveller who explored many parts of Northern Arabia, tried in 1805–1806 to reach Petra, which no doubt was known simply as Wadi Musa. He went from Mount Sinai to Hebron and had apparently no suspicion of the existence of the long valley of the Jordan Rift. In 1812 Burckhardt was on his way from Damascus to Cairo. He knew of Seetzen's failure, for more than once he seems to have employed a guide who had been with Seetzen. The first mention that he makes in his Journal of the matter is when on August 22 he writes that he was particularly desirous of visiting Wadi Musa " and its antiquities," of which he had heard the country-people speak with great admiration. He wished to go straight from the Wadi Musa to Cairo, avoiding Aqaba, but his guide insisted that he must go by the longer route. He says: " The road from Shobek to Akaba, which is tolerably good, and might easily be rendered practical even to artillery, lies to the east of the Wadi Musa, and to have quitted it out of mere curiosity to see the Wadi would have looked suspicious in the eyes of the Arabs. I, therefore, pretended to have made a vow to have slaughtered a goat in honour of Haroun, whose tomb I knew was situated at the extremity of the valley, and by this stratagem I thought that I should have the means of seeing the valley on my way to the tomb. To this my guide had nothing to oppose; the dread of drawing upon himself, by resistance, the wrath of Haroun completely silenced him." He finds a camp of Fallahin " who lay up the produce of their harvest in a kind of fortress called Oerak, where are a few houses surrounded by a stone wall." From here he " ascends a mountain " and travels some time along its barren summit in a south-west direction, and then descends and reaches the spring Ain Musa, which is some two or three miles east of Alji. He notes that on the " summit of the mountain the road to Wadi Musa diverges from the great road to Akaba," and here he was pressed to make his sacrifice (Jabal Harun being visible in the distance) as former pilgrims had done.

At Alji he finds an Arab who will be his guide for Jabal Harun and will carry the goat and a skin of water. He says: " Here the antiquities of the Wadi Musa begin," but cannot stop for exploration because of the suspiciousness of his guide, though he notes the three Sahrij monuments and the Obelisk Tomb, goes through the Siq, and gives a fairly accurate sketch ground-plan of the interior of the Khazna. He saw some of the tombs in the Outer Siq, and must have been specially guided by his Arab to the particular one which contains twelve graves (Fig. 100), for it is somewhat far on the right from any ordinary route through the Outer Siq, and, therefore, would only have been reached if he had been specially told of it. He sees the Urn Tomb and the Corinthian, and crosses over Petra to the Qasr al Bint. He is told that the water of the Wadi Musa in the Siyagh runs underground for a quarter of a mile. Here he is threatened by his Arab as a treasure-hunter because he has so much curiosity about the insides of the monuments. He continues southwards, however, along the Thughra Wadi until he reaches the terrace below al Barra, from which the mountain can be seen. Here it is already sunset, and he is not unnaturally " excessively fatigued," so that he has to kill his goat here in sight of the mountain but without ever reaching it. He has to return at once as best he can to Alji. He says in conclusion: " In comparing the testimony of the authors cited in Reland's *Palaestina,** it appears very probable that the ruins in Wadi Musa are those of the ancient Petra, and it is remarkable that Eusebius says that the tomb of Aaron was shown near Petra."

I have examined Reland's book carefully throughout, but I do not find a word in it about the existence of " monuments " of any sort at Petra.

Reland is very minute in his work, and so conscientious that he devotes many pages in his second volume (which is in the form of a Gazetteer) to justify his inclusion of any mention of Petra at all in a treatise on Palestine. He concludes, however, that it may properly be considered as part of " Palaestina tertia," and in a list of bishops in that region, under the name of Petra, adds " Stephanus ἐν ἐθνικοῖς (*i.e.*, ' in partibus ') attribuit Palaestina III. 111.''

In the 52 pages which he gives to Petra in his second volume, after a few in which he justifies its inclusion at all, the whole of the remainder (48 pages) is taken up by the reproduction of a letter from M. Jacques de Bary, containing a learned discussion on coins, with a number of illustrations, but without any reference to the place itself or anything in it. The only authors whom Reland quotes are Pliny, Strabo, Eusebius, etc., and they are only quoted in reference to Petra being really properly included as an Urbs Palaestinae. I am, therefore, entirely at a loss to understand Burckhardt's reference to them. Among the mountains of Perea Mount Hor is not even mentioned.

Reland gives the longitude of Petra (p. 463) as $66\frac{11}{24}$ (which is obviously in Ptolemaic reckoning), instead of 35° 27'. His latitude of $30\frac{1}{3}$ is correct.

Burckhardt continues: " Of this at least I am persuaded, from all the information I procured, that there is no other ruin between the extremities of the Dead Sea and Red Sea of sufficient importance to answer to that city. Whether or no I have discovered the remains of the capital of Arabia Petraea, I leave to the decision of Greek scholars." He notes that there are a great many tombs, but, of course, has no time to look at them. He speaks of " at least 250 sepulchres " belonging to different periods. Then he goes to Alji and Ma'an and so to Aqaba and then to Cairo. He includes in his note a little sketch-map which, although very inaccurate, was better than anything else that was in existence, and gives an odd sketch of a Nabataean monument, as it seems to have impressed his memory, in the shape of a somewhat flat triangle, three or four times as broad at the base as at the top, and having a pilaster sloping up on the edge of each of its two oblique sides. This notion of obliquity must, I think, have been based upon a recollection of the sloping sides of the excavation that had so generally to be made in the mountain side in order to get a vertical face for the monuments, for there are certainly no monuments of anything like the shape which he sketched.

Burton says,† in describing his visit to Cairo:

" Here lies the Swiss Burckhardt, who enjoyed a wonderful immunity from censure until a

---

* Reland, *Palaestina ex monumentis veteribus illustrata*, 1714 (2 vols., sm. 4to.).
† Burton, *Pilgrimage to Al Madinah and Mecca*, Vol. I., p. 84.

certain pseudo-Orientalist of the present day seized the opportunity of using the ' unscrupulous traveller's ' information and of abusing his memory.   Some years ago, the sum of £20 (I am informed) was collected in order to raise a fitting monument over the discoverer of Petra's humble grave.   Some objection, however, was started, because Moslems are supposed to claim Burckhardt as one of their own saints.   Only hear the Egyptian account of his death !   After returning from al Hijaz, he taught Tajwid (Koran chaunting) in the Azhar mosque, where the learned, suspecting him to be at heart an infidel, examined his person, and found the formula of the Muhammadan faith written in token of abhorrence upon the soles of his feet.   Thereupon, the principal of the Mosque, in a transport of holy indignation, did decapitate him with one blow of the sword.   It only remains to be observed, that nothing can be more ridiculous than the popular belief, except it be our hesitating to offend the prejudices of such believers."

Burckhardt's account of his adventures was published after his death by Murray in 1822, under the title of *Travels in Syria and the Holy Land.*

In 1829 Mr. David Roberts, R.A., was able to spend sufficient time in Petra to make the drawings which were among those afterwards published in three folio volumes (1849) under the title of *The Holy Land, Syria, Idumea, Arabia,* etc.   Roberts does not seem to have been attracted at all by the more ancient monuments, but only by those which were distinctly classical in their origin.   His fourteen drawings of these are beautiful examples of draughtsmanship, and as regards the architectural details their accuracy is wonderful, considering the very small number of days which he had at his disposal.   As regards the scenery, his treatment of the rocks is entirely conventional, and gives no idea of what the place is like, but his views of the Palace, the Dair, and the Khazna leave nothing to be desired.   The text which accompanies Roberts' drawings is entirely valueless, but some particulars as to his journey are given in a little book by Mr. Kinnear, who was one of his companions.*

Viscount Castlereagh, M.P., spent as much as four days in Petra in 1842, and describes how he ascended the heights above the theatre, where he found " some ruins with an excavation resembling a large shallow tank and two very insignificant obelisks, all more or less in ruins."   Apparently he must have been looking at what is recognised as a very perfect place of sacrifice (Fig. 163) without recognising in any way its significance.

The only other very early visit to Petra the results of which have any interest, is one made by two gentlemen who were Commanders in the Royal Navy (the Hon. C. L. Irby and Mr. James Mangles) and spent two years in travelling in the East.   They published their Journal for private distribution in 1823 under the title of *Travels in Egypt and Nubia, Syria and Asia Minor during the years 1817 and 1818.*   These explorers arrived at Petra from the west and north in May, 1818, passing Shaubak on their way, and having endless troubles with the Alji people and other Arabs. They apparently crossed north of al Nasara and reached al Khan (p. 43).   They mention here colossal lions on each side of the entrance, much decayed, as to which see p. 44.†   They visit the Qasr al Bint and examine the " house " of Fig. 134, noting that the fourth window lights the upper room only, a fact which no subsequent visitors seem to have noted.   They speak of a river flowing in the Wadi Musa with considerable rapidity.   They spend two long days in general exploration, seeing the Palace and the Corinthian Tomb and the Urn Temple, as well as the Serpent Monument on the south.   On their last day they were able to make an ascent of Mount Hor. They describe it as toilsome, having had in many places to proceed on hands and knees.   From the top of Mount Hor they saw the upper part of the Dair Monument (Fig. 23), to which afterwards

* *Cairo, Petra, and Damascus in 1839,* London, 1841.
† *Cf.* the animal-looking naturally weathered buttresses of Br. 195 in Fig. 109.

they tried fruitlessly to find a route from the valley.   They eventually left Petra by the direct north route to Shaubak, finding the weather on May 26 excessively cold.

From some point reached by scrambling up a difficult gorge from the Khazna, where they had to use their hands nearly as much as their feet, they say they found some small pyramids hewn out of the rock on the summit of the heights, and discovered also " a much higher conical point on the mountain, to whose summit there is a regular spiral staircase of ascent cut with great care and neatness."   They also saw from the same point the Urn on the top of the Dair, which they saw afterwards from Mount Hor.   In the small sketch-map which they publish, the " conical point " is shown in the middle of the open valley between Numair and al Barra—that is, somewhere south of the position of the Serpent Monument.   No such isolated peak exists, still less any spiral road, so that one cannot identify what it was that gave the visitors this impression.   One can only suggest that it must have been Jabal Numair, but misplaced when the map was drawn.   Everywhere, however, in the rocks round Petra there are regular terraces of great length and regularity, which may well have been taken for artificially made roads, especially under certain conditions of light.

These two naval officers seem to have seen a great deal of Petra, and by no means to have confined themselves to looking at the two or three show places which for the next three-quarters of a century came to be nearly all at which the casual visitor ever thought of looking.   Travelling, however, in their time cannot have been a joy, for—apart altogether from many adventures and troubles, and a dangerous attack of fever, the story ends—" Towards the middle of December, it was too late to renew our attempts in Karamania, and as we were much enfeebled by illness we embarked for Marseilles in a French brig of 120 tons, and after a passage of seventy-six days during constant gales of wind, we reached that place, where we performed a quarantine of twenty days, and then proceeded to Montpellier to recruit our health."

The large number of visitors who published their recollections or experiences during the remainder of the century have, with very few exceptions, confined themselves to looking at, and admiring—or criticising, as they felt inclined—the half-dozen most notable classical monuments, and when this duty was performed, to spend the rest of their time and pen and ink in a most unchristian rejoicing—one may, in fact, say, a pious chortling—over the fact that Edom was cursed in the Old Testament, that Petra was part of Edom, and that the curses have come home to roost. Nowhere have I found any recognition of the fact that the wickedness of the Edomites seems to have been exactly the same as the wickedness of the Belgians in 1914 in objecting to the passage through their own country of a foreign army.   Apart from this radical question, however, apparently only two or three of these good people have recognised that the iniquity of the Edomites, whatever it may have been, was certainly followed by over 1,000 years of great prosperity for their successors, and that the present ruin caused by the desiccation of the whole country only took place some centuries even after it had been in the occupation of the Romans, whose ancestors cannot very well have had anything to do with the refusal of one ancient Semitic tribe to allow another warlike Semitic tribe to traverse its country.   Be that as it may, the genially-minded visitors to Petra during the nineteenth century devote very frequently many more pages to their satisfaction at what they call the " fulfilment of prophecy " than they do to the description of what they might have seen by opening their eyes and looking round them—only two or three of them, in fact, ever do seem to have opened their eyes and looked round them at all.   One good gentleman even finds considerable corroboration of prophetical fulfilment in the falling of a scorpion on to his bed !   I think it was this same gentleman who, after pluckily reaching the obelisk ridge by the route of the ledge (Fig. 208), sees the obelisks and the ruins of the fortification, but absolutely does not see, or, at least, does not mention, the place of sacrifice upon which, or within a few yards of which, he was actually standing. But it is only fair to him and others to say that from my own experience the whole terrain once covered by the ancient city is so complicated that one may be making a second or third visit to a particular spot before one sees something that has been staring one right in the face every time.

Of these other nineteenth-century visitors there are two or three who ought to be mentioned. Miss Martineau, in her *Eastern Life: Past and Present*, describes a visit of three days in 1847, and tells also how she and some of her companions wandered over a large part of the Petraean area north of the Wadi Musa, and were greatly impressed with the enormous number of the Nabataean tombs or monuments, of which scarcely anybody else took the trouble to recognise even the existence. She speaks of their number being thousands, which naturally is an exaggeration. She gives also a vivid description of a spate in the Wadi Musa in March, 1847 (see p. 53).

Dr. Robinson also, who had only one complete day in the place, but employed it very fully (1838), notices that the whole valley is full of ruins, and expresses his wonder that his predecessors have said nothing about this. Laborde also was one who certainly saw and noted the Nabataean monuments.

Mr. Chichester Hart, who went out as botanist with Hull in 1883, describes the flora of Petra in chapter vii. of his *Naturalist's Journey to Sinai*, etc.

A tendency to look only at the classical monuments seems to have been so extraordinarily strong that even a visitor like Mr. E. L. Wilson, whose chief interest in Petra was that of a photographer, has nothing to say about the Nabataean monuments, except to describe them as having " numerous, tapering, and receding façades "—a description which, as the photographs show, is singularly inaccurate. He found blind fish in the cistern on the Obelisk Ridge, and visited also the great tank above the Farasa Temple. He gives a drawing of the circular altar at the place of sacrifice, but does not seem to think much of what appears to be the principal one.

I am afraid it must be confessed with shame that a considerable number of the English-speaking visitors speak with pride of finding the names of former Englishmen or Americans scratched or chalked on the walls of the monuments. One gentleman even goes so far as to point out that it is only English-speaking people who are civilised and educated enough to do this !

A clear and consecutive chronology is not one of the many and great merits of that noble work *Arabia Deserta*, but it seems certain from Mr. Doughty's preface to his second edition that he had visited Petra before his great expedition of 1876, although we have no record of what he saw or thought of it. During that expedition, however, he tells us that he left the pilgrims somewhere, I think, about Ma'an, in order to pay another visit to Petra. He speaks of reaching the " rocky coomb-land " between Shaubak and Petra, and thence going southwards towards the Wadi Musa, naturally avoiding Alji altogether. As he descends he sees far off under the sun Qasr Fir'un—that is, the only building in the valley of Petra which is of regular masonry. " In this country every marvel is ascribed to Pharaoh, who made himself, they tell me, to be worshipped as a god, and here resisted Moses and Aaron." He stopped for the night under a little hewn cistern, which he calls " Ain Musa "—not, of course, the Ain Musa which is some three miles east of Alji. With some companions he started next morning, failed to persuade the Arabs to go to Mount Hor, but turned up into the Siq, near the mouth of which " is that most perfect of the monuments, Khasna Faraoun, whose sculptured columns and cornices are pure lines of a crystalline beauty without blemish, whereupon the golden sun looks from above, and Nature has painted that sand rock ruddy with iron rust."

He camps somewhere in the Bab-al-Siq, and returns the next day " to view the rest of the monuments of Petra."

" Upon a tomb in the west cliffs of three columns, whose hewn fore-wall is broken away beneath, I saw a large, perfect, and beautiful ancient inscription of several lines. It might be Nabataean." (No doubt the Turkamaniya, Fig. 104.)

He gives a very rough sketch of what is obviously intended for the front of the Turkamaniya monument, and adds: "An hour from the Siq is said to be another inscription (above a hewn casement in the rock) at a place called Sabra. Strange and horrible as a pit in the inhuman deadness of nature is this site of the Nabataeans' metropolis. The eye recoils from that mountainous close of iron cliffs, in which the ghastly waste monuments of a sumptuous barbaric art are from the first glance an eyesore."

He was then taken up to see the Dair, which he left at sunset, and reached his mule again at the Khazna Fir'un, and would have camped at Alji if the villagers had not been so very antagonistic that he had to pass by them. He did not, therefore, have very much opportunity of seeing anything in Petra, and it is clear from the quotations which I have given in another chapter that his great object was the finding of inscriptions.

As a set-off against the very severe quotation which I have just made, one must also add that later on, speaking particularly of the much less impressive monuments at Madaïn Salih, he says: " No one can consider without emotion the severe and proud lineaments of these solemn ranges of caverns."

Among the few visitors to Petra who have added something to our knowledge of the place ought to be named Drs. Libbey and Hoskins,* who first noticed the existence of the " High Place " behind al Habis, of which the triclinium of Fig. 139 is the most striking part. These gentlemen call al Habis the " Citadel Rock." In their plate, on p. 203, " Eastward " should read " Westward."

The scientific exploration of Petra dates only from the commencement of the present century. The earliest visitor whose work remains valuable was Professor Alois Musil. His first visit to Petra appears to have been in 1896, but his researches were not published until 1907, when they formed volume ii. of his *Arabia Petraea*. He acknowledges that by this time he had the advantage of the work done by Brünnow in the early part of the century, and of his maps, which were published in 1904. Musil deals at considerable length with the classical monuments. He very specially visited and describes places of cult, such as the ridge above the Turkamaniya Wadi (afterwards fully dealt with by Dalman), and other similar places on the Ma'aisara ridges. He investigated several Holy Places on the route to the Dair, as well as on the Dair plateau. He also visited the places of cult at al Qantara and at al Madras, as well as those on the top of al Khubdha. He examined very thoroughly the remains of old fortifications at Wu'aira and on the Obelisk Ridge. He made a successful ascent of Mount Hor, and gives photographs. Oddly enough, although he was a most diligent explorer, he says very little indeed about the Nabataean monuments, and shows them only in his Fig. 87, which he calls a part of al Barra, but which is in reality a part of the face of al Biyara. (His Figures 89 and 92 have also been accidentally wrongly located.) In speaking of the Nabataean monuments he uses Brünnow's nomenclature entirely without any remarks. This part of his work must, therefore, have been written after the publication of Brünnow's book.

The most valuable work on Petra which has yet appeared is, beyond all question, volume i. of *Die Provincia Arabia*, by Brünnow and Domaszewski, published in 1904. These two Professors, along with Euting, the Epigraphist, and apparently quite a large party, spent ten days at Petra in March, 1897, and a fortnight in March of the subsequent year. Their great work was a detailed examination of the positions of over 800 monuments of different kinds, the scheduling of all these

* *The Jordan Valley and Petra*, 2 vols., 1905 (Vol. II., p. 191).

E

objects, and the showing of their positions upon eighteen maps, generally on a scale of $\frac{3}{10,000}$, or about 19 inches per mile. The maps also show elaborate contours, but these latter unfortunately are to a very large extent imaginary, and the aeroplane surveys show that they do not even approximately represent the irregularities of the surface. The schedule of monuments and their placing on the maps is, however, sufficiently complete, and so far accurate as to make possible an examination of the whole place in a way which, before the existence of these maps, or without their use, would have been entirely out of the question. The book is unfortunately difficult to obtain, and exceedingly bulky. I myself photographed the whole of the maps, and had them mounted separately so that each one could be carried easily in a pocket. In this form they proved invaluable in moving about the place. It is not to be pretended that the position of every monument is quite accurately shown, but in nearly every instance it can be identified, which is all that is necessary. These investigators employed themselves specially in classifying the different monuments according to the characteristics of their external façades. This, unfortunately—or, perhaps, fortunately for future explorers—led to their almost total neglect of an immense number of monuments which have no façades, or of which the original fronts have been so weathered away or otherwise destroyed as to be unrecognisable.

Brünnow has attached to his list of monuments a nomenclature which, to my regret, I have not found it possible to accept. As I have said above, he disregards altogether what apparently are the very oldest of the Petraean monuments, and does not classify them in any way. To the earlier Nabataean monuments he gives the general name of "Pylon." The chief characteristics of a pylon, as applied in Egyptian architecture, are that it is an isolated block, rectangular, but not square, in section, and very much larger in area in the lower part than in the upper, so that its sides are, at any rate for a great portion of its height, sloping inwards. The ordinary Nabataean monument, carved in a cliff wall, is, of course, by hypothesis not isolated, and the cases in which its sides depart from parallelism, or approximate parallelism, are very few indeed. To the type of monument to which I have given the name of "corniced," Brünnow has given the title "Stufengrab," which is obviously sufficiently applicable, but is applicable also to all the other monuments which have crowsteps. The later and more developed façades Brünnow calls "Hegrs" and "Proto-hegrs," according to their development. "Hegr" (more correctly Hajar, or, perhaps, Hujar) is merely an Arabic word for chambers or caves, and is therefore in fact more directly applicable to the simple "pylons" than to the later monuments. But the same word (*cf.* Ptolemy's Egra) is also the original Arabic name, and still the vulgar name, of Madaïn Salih. It is possible that at the time when Brünnow was at work the dates of the actual Madaïn Salih tombs had not been so thoroughly ascertained as they have been since, and they may have been taken for the parents instead of the children of Petra. Under these conditions I have, therefore, felt myself compelled with some regret to adopt a nomenclature entirely different from that adopted by Brünnow. In order to facilitate future study of the monuments, I have in the text always referred to monuments to which Brünnow has given a number by that number.

There has, unfortunately, been a great difference of opinion between the principal explorers as to the names of the different parts of Petra and its neighbourhood. The names which I have used in the text of this book have been those which I think, after looking into the matter, are probably the most nearly accurate. In particular it will be noted that Brünnow adopts the name of "acropolis" for the little isolated rock to the west of Qasr al Bint, of which apparently the proper title is al Habis. The latter name Brünnow gives in error to the great mass of al Biyara, which is separated from al Habis by the Thughra Wadi.

In the third volume of *Die Provincia Arabia* Brünnow gives a review of the history of the provinces for the first seven centuries A.D., and later he also gives a very complete chronological table of events connected with the provinces from the time of Augustus onwards, and gives, further, a bibliographical appendix bringing the record of Petraean literature in his first volume up to date. In his first volume (pp. 15 to 125) he also gives a full description of several routes from Jerusalem to Petra, with illustrations. The method of getting to Petra, however, now that the Hijaz Railway is more or less available, is of course much easier than it was when the whole distance from Jerusalem had to be covered on horseback or camelback.

A particularly useful feature of Brünnow's schedule of monuments is that for all the principal ones he gives very full extracts from the descriptions of earlier travellers who have seen and noted them—descriptions which are not only historically interesting, but which illustrate very markedly the way in which appreciation of these antiquities has modified itself during the last hundred years.

Brünnow's book is profusely illustrated with well-chosen illustrations. Unfortunately, in my own copy and other copies which I have seen, the blocks are so much over-printed that their details are in many cases not legible at all. It is to be hoped that if the book is to be republished some day, as it may well be, trouble will be taken to give the illustrations the treatment which they really deserve.

The third and latest work of special importance in connection with Petra is that of Dr. Dalman, *Petra und Seine Felsheiligtumer (1908)* and *Neue Petraforschungen (1912)* (Leipzig). Dr. Dalman's work was done, and very thoroughly done, in a number of visits which he made with a large party within the years 1896 to 1907. His principal volume being published in 1908, he had already before him in writing it, and in fact also during at least some of his visits, the work which had been already done by Brünnow. Indeed, without that work his own work would have been very greatly more difficult than it was. One cannot help regretting that in spite of this fact the author seems to take a positive delight in finding as many mistakes, or alleged mistakes, in Brünnow's work as he possibly can, and spends pages over minute and rather fierce criticisms of matters which are not of the slightest importance.

Dalman's object in working at Petra was quite different from that of his predecessors. He was the President of the " Deutsch Evangelische Institut für Altertumswissenschaft des Heiligen Landes " in Jerusalem. His position, therefore, naturally gave him special interest in all the monuments or places in Petra which were, or could have been, connected with religious worship of any kind, and his work is confined practically to an enumeration and discussion of these places. He has himself been the discoverer of a large number of " Holy Places," and he gives detailed descriptions of them with references to their position on his map, and accompanies these descriptions in many cases with useful detailed sketches as well as photographs.

There are certainly many places of cult to be found in Petra beyond those included in his list, but his work has covered by far the greater number of such places as come under his own definition. (See Chapter IV., § v.) He does his best in the text of his work to indicate the sort of way in which the Holy Places might have been used in the cult of the Nabataeans, but it is to be admitted that what can be said with any certainty, even by such a diligent explorer, amounts to very little. Among other conclusions to which he comes, one is that very probably those Holy Places described by him in which the rocks have been made use of to the greatest extent in their natural shapes and in which the smallest amount of artificial work has been done on them are the oldest. How old they may be neither he nor any other investigator has been able to tell us. It is to be hoped that more light will be thrown on this particular point when the authorities have allowed digging to be carried out at Petra.   He argues very strongly—partly on the grounds just mentioned—that the much-visited High Place on the Obelisk Ridge (Fig. 163) can by no means have been the original and chief Holy Place of Petra.   I do not gather that he has formed any very definite opinion as to whether the obelisks formed in any way part of some still older cult.   He thinks, however, for various reasons that the great High Place dates only from the time of King Aretas III. in the last century B.C.

In addition to his descriptions and discussions on the Holy Places, his work contains interesting chapters of a general nature on the position and fortification of the original city and its probable commercial conditions, as well as on the pains which the inhabitants had taken to provide themselves with water in all circumstances.

He adds a chapter on what little is known as to the early history of the Nabataeans.

It is interesting to note that he himself has found in Petra 180 idol blocks in different monuments or places, as to which he says that not one was within a chamber which was certainly a grave.

I do not think that even Dr. Dalman has realised the very small proportion of façades of classical type among the whole of those in Petra—only one in twenty-five or thirty of those of the Nabataean type.

While this book has been in preparation at least three works concerning Petra have been published. A number of a periodical called *Wonders of the Past*, undated, but published, I think, in 1922, contains some large and very well-printed Petraean photographs, chiefly, of course, as in all the other instances, of the classical monuments.

The Reverend A. Forder, whose long residence in Trans-Jordan has enabled him to make very many visits to Petra, has published a book called *Petra, Perea, and Phoenicia*, which contains a large number of exceedingly good and well-printed photographs of Petra and its monuments, the subjects being unusually well chosen.   For some reason which I do not understand the author seems in his text to be making fun of his readers to a very large extent.

Still more recently there has also been published the *Vanished Cities of Arabia* by Mrs. Steuart Erskine, in which she deals with Petra, Karak, Madaba, Amman, Jarash, and some other places.   Her visit to Petra was a very short one, but she gives a number of historical details of the position of the Nabataeans in the Herodian period, by which time I am afraid they had lost interest to us as rock carvers.   Petra, having once gained the name of the " Rose-red City," will, I suppose, always possess it; but visitors who are attracted by the brilliancy of colouring of Mr. Fletcher's pictures in Mrs. Erskine's book should be warned that the colours which he depicts are certainly not those which they will see when they get to Petra.

CHAPTER III

THE NABATAEANS AND THEIR SUCCESSORS

THE Nabataeans, the people to whom we owe the bulk of the rock-carvings of Petra, were a Semitic tribe, originally, if Diodorus is to be trusted (which may be doubtful), nomadic Badawin with very little civilisation. They came apparently from Arabia, east of what is to-day called Trans-Jordan (the *Oultre-Jourdain* of the Crusaders), and may have taken possession of the country of the Edomites, either by the normal Oriental plan of forcible seizure, or by peaceful occupation after the Edomites had moved westward to the richer lands of the Mediterranean (587 B.C.). They can little have anticipated that, as appears to be the view of many (otherwise) kindly and well-disposed Christian people, they would bring themselves by this movement under a divine curse. The curse, however, fell eventually not upon them, but on the Romans, a still further remove from the wicked Edomites who had originally earned it.

Practically nothing certain is known of their early history. In the time of Assur-bani-pal they had been powerful enough to require to be dealt with by that gentle monarch, and their inclusion in the list of his enemies in a campaign of 647-6 B.C. is apparently the first definite historical mention of them which we have. (See also Chapter II.)

After Alexander's occupation of Egypt some of his generals twice attacked Petra, about 310 B.C. By that time Petra had become a place which could be looted, so that the tribe, if originally nomadic, must have altered its customs and to some extent settled down. Diodorus is very uncomplimentary to the Nabataeans, and especially scornful about their possession of mercantile instincts which prevented them from being good fighters. They are certainly said to have bought off the second Greek attack by a large payment. But whether they fought well or not they managed somehow to prevent the Greek army from occupying their city, and afterwards lived there in unmolested possession for centuries, becoming later on a sort of semi-independent dependency of Rome, until, in A.D. 106, Trajan took over the whole kingdom.

Arabs from the east of Jordan appear to have taken some part—chiefly as bandits—in the Jewish revolution of A.D. 66, but I find no special mention of the Nabataeans as helping the revolutionaries in any such way as to bring them at that time under the wrath of the Romans. Robertson Smith (*Ency. Brit.*) says they " were a chief element in the disorders which invited Pompey's intervention in Jerusalem " (*circa* 50 B.C.).

In the time of Paul (see 2 Cor. xi. 32) a Nabataean king (Aretas IV.) was at Damascus, and the Nabataean inscriptions at Madaïn Salih show that during the first century of our era the Nabataean Kingdom extended as far south as that place, a distance from Damascus of nearly 600 miles. Immediately south of Madaïn Salih (only a few miles away), Lihyanite inscriptions alone are found, and although the tombs are still of the Petraean type, their writers no longer celebrate their Nabataean king " loving his people."

Two classical writers only—Diodorus Siculus and Strabo—writing at about the same date (not many years before our era), give us any particulars about the Nabataeans, and it is worth while (as the originals are not very readily accessible) to give a translation of their statements.

Diodorus may possibly have been speaking rather of what he supposed the Nabataeans to have

been at the time of the Greek attacks than of what he knew them to be in his own days. His story*
is as follows:

"Antigonus, having without danger regained the whole of Syria and Phoenicia, undertook an
expedition to the region of the Arabs who are called Nabataei. Judging this race to be alien to his
own interests, he chose out from his friends Athenaeus; and committing to him 4,000 light-armed
infantry and 600 cavalry well fitted for speed, he ordered him to attack the barbarians suddenly and
take from them all their cattle. Here it is worth while, for the sake of those ignorant of it, to recount
the institutions of these Arabs, by the practice of which they seem to protect their liberty. They
pass their life in the open air, giving the name of ' their country ' to that solitude, devoid of inhabitants,
which has neither rivers nor copious springs from which it is possible for a hostile army to get water.
They have a law neither to sow corn nor to plant any fruit-bearing plant, nor to use wine nor to build
a house; and whoever is found acting in a contrary way is adjudged the punishment of death. This
law they hold because they judge that those who possess these things will be easily compelled by
powerful men to do what is ordered them because of their enjoyment of these things. Some of
them keep camels, others sheep, pasturing them over the desert. Of the Arabian tribes there are
not a few who graze the desert, and these are much superior to the others in the amenities of life,
being in number not much more than 10,000. For not a few of them are wont to bring down to
the sea frankincense and myrrh and the most costly of the spices, receiving them from those who
convey them from what is called Arabia Felix. They are conspicuously lovers of freedom, and
when a strong force of the enemy approaches, they flee into the desert, using this as a stronghold.
For since it suffers from want of water it is inaccessible to the others, but to these alone who have
provided pitched earthen vessels, buried beneath the earth, it affords a safe refuge. For since the
land is argillaceous and has soft rock, they make great caves in it, the mouths of which they make
quite small, but, ever increasing the width of them deep down, they at last render the size so great
that each side measures a plethrum. They fill those vessels with rain-water and block up the mouths
(of the caves), and, making them flush with the rest of the land, they leave signals there which are
known to themselves, but not understood by anyone else.

"They water their cattle every three days, lest while fleeing in waterless places they should
require to be watered every day. Their own food is meat and milk and such edible things as spring
from the ground. Pepper grows among them, and much of what is called wild honey comes from
the trees, which they use mixed with water as a drink. There are also other races of Arabs, some
of whom till the ground, mingling with the tributaries, and have some features in common with the
Syrians, except the living in houses.

"These, then, are found to be the manners and customs of the Arabians; and there being near
to them a great fair held to which the neighbours were wont to resort, some to sell their wares, others
to buy anything they had use for, they journeyed to this, leaving in a rock their possessions, and their
oldest men, along with their children and wives. Now that place was extremely strong, but without
walls, and distant from the inhabited part a two days' journey.

"Athenaeus and his men, then, carefully noting this time, set out for the Rock with his force
in light order, and having, in their march from the province of Idumaea for three days and three
nights, covered 2,200 stades, about midnight seized the Rock without being observed by the Arabs,
and forthwith of those taken therein some they killed, others they took alive, and some who were
wounded they left, and of the frankincense and myrrh they packed up and carried off the greater
part, and about 500 talents of silver, and not staying longer than a watch they immediately returned

* Diodorus XIX. 94-7.

with haste, judging that they would be pursued by the barbarians, and having traversed 200 stades they returned to camp quite tired out; and they kept the watches carelessly, thinking that the enemy could not come within two or three days. But the Arabs, being informed by those who had seen the camp, immediately assembled, and, leaving the fair, came to the Rock. Learning there from the wounded what had happened they in all haste pursued the Greeks, and because the soldiers of Athenaeus were camping negligently, and, on account of their weariness were buried in sleep, some of the captives ran away unobserved, from whom the Nabataeans, learning the state of the enemy, attacked the camp about the third watch, not less than 8,000 in number, and most of them they slaughtered while still in their beds, but those who woke up and were flying to arms they shot down. In the end the infantry were all killed, but of the cavalry upwards of fifty got safe off, and of these most were wounded. Athenaeus' men then, while they succeeded at first, afterwards, on account of their own imprudence, met with disaster in this way. For slackness and contempt are commonly wont to follow successes. Wherefore some very properly infer that it is easier to bear disasters well than great successes with prudence. For the former (calamities) compel men, on account of their fear for the future, to careful management, but the latter, on account of the foregone success, induce men to despise everything.

" But the Nabataeans, having chastised their enemies like men, themselves returned to the Rock, having set their affairs in order, and sending a letter to Antigonus written in Syriac letters, accused Athenaeus, making excuses for themselves. Antigonus wrote back to them, confessing that they had justly avenged themselves, and accused Athenaeus, alleging that the attack had been made by him contrary to the orders given him. This he did in order to conceal his policy, wishing to inveigle the barbarians into slackness, that after attacking them he might succeed beyond his hopes in his enterprise. For it was not easy without craft to overcome men who had chosen a nomad life, and who had the desert as an inaccessible refuge. The Arabs were much delighted, because they seemed to have been freed from great fears; yet they did not altogether trust the words of Antigonus, but keeping their hopes ambiguous they posted lookouts on the hills from which it was easy to see from afar any incursions into Arabia. And themselves, after settling their own affairs, waited to see what would happen. Then Antigonus having proposed friendship for the barbarians for a time, and thinking that they, being taken in, had offered a good opportunity against them, selected from his whole force 4,000 armed infantry, light-armed and good at speed, and more than 4,000 cavalry, and these he ordered to bring with them food (not needing fire) for several days, and having appointed Demetrius, his son, leader, he sent them off in the first watch with the order to inflict punishment on the Arabs in whatever way he could. He then, marching for three days through pathless places, hastened to entrap the barbarians.

" But the scouts, perceiving an enemy force invading them, signalled to the Nabataeans by means of the torches agreed upon. Therefore the barbarians, thinking that the Greeks were coming shortly, deposited their belongings in the Rock, and set over it a sufficient guard, there being only one way up, made by hand. But themselves having divided the booty, rode off by different routes into the desert. When he (Demetrius) came to the Rock, and perceived that the booty had been removed, he made continuous attacks on the place, and when those inside defended themselves vigorously, and easily prevailed on account of the strength of the position, he then, after continuing the struggle till evening, gave the signal for a retreat. On the next day, when he again brought up his forces to the Rock, one of the barbarians cried out: ' O King Demetrius, what do you want, or what induces you to make war with us, who live in a solitude, and places which have neither water, nor corn, nor wine, nor absolutely any of those things that among you are considered necessities.

We, refusing to admit of slavery on any terms, have fled for refuge into a country in want of all those things necessary to others, and chosen to live a life solitary and altogether wild, doing no harm to you. We beg, therefore, both you and your father not to wrong us, but after taking gifts from us to lead off your army, and to consider the Nabataeans your friends for the future. For even if you wish it you cannot stay here many days, being in want of water and all other necessaries; nor can you compel us to love another life; but you will only have some captives as slaves with dejected minds and men who could not endure to live under other laws.' When such speeches had been made, Demetrius, leading away his army, bade them send ambassadors about these matters, and the Arabs sent their eldest men, who, saying much the same as what has been already stated, persuaded (Demetrius) to accept such gifts as are most precious among them, and to put an end to the whole business."

In another place* Diodorus makes the following statement about the Nabataean people and their country:

" These matters having been thus set forth by us, our story will now turn to the other parts of Asia not yet described, and particularly Arabia. This country lies between Syria and Egypt, and is divided between many and various races. The eastern parts are inhabited by the Arabians, whom they call Nabataeans, who dwell in a country partly desert, partly waterless, and a small part fertile. They live a predatory life, and raid and harry much of the neighbouring country, and in wars they are hard to beat. For in what is called the Waterless Region they have wells sunk in convenient places, keeping the knowledge of them from other tribes, and in this region they take refuge with impunity. For since they themselves know the hidden places of the waters they open up these and enjoy plenty of drink. But as to the strangers who are pursuing them, being without water on account of their ignorance of the wells, some perish on account of want of water, and others, after suffering much distress, reach their home again with difficulty. For this reason the Arabs who inhabit this region, since they cannot be reduced by war, continue to be free men, and, in addition to this, they never admit a ruler from outside, but maintain their freedom unshaken for ever. Therefore, neither the Assyrians of old, nor the Medes and Persians, nor, further, the Kings of the Macedonians were able to subdue them; though they brought many great forces against them they never succeeded in bringing their enterprises to a successful issue.

" Now there is also in the region of the Nabataeans a rock excessively strong with only one way up, and going up by this way in small parties they deposit their baggage.

" Moreover, there is a large lake which produces much bitumen, from which they derive no small revenue. Now this lake has a length of about 500 stades, and a breadth of about 60 stades. The water has an evil smell and is very bitter, so it cannot support fish or any other of the usual water animals. Though great rivers of remarkable sweetness flow into it, yet none the less it swamps this sweetness by virtue of its malodorousness. From the midst of it every year a great mass of bitumen wells up, sometimes more than three plethra broad, and sometimes two. Wherefore the barbarians who dwell round about usually call the greater gush a " Bull " and the smaller a " Calf." When the bitumen floods the land like a sea, the place appears to those who view it from a distance like an island. Now so it comes to pass that the coming of the eruption of the bitumen becomes clear to the men twenty days before. For all round the lake to a distance of many stades, a stench falls upon them in a great blast, and all the silver and gold and bronze in the district loses its natural colour; but this is regained when all the bitumen has been ejected. The neighbouring region being fiery and malodorous afflicts men's bodies with disease and makes them altogether short-lived.

* Diodorus II. 48.

" But the land is good for the growth of (date-) palms, as much of it as is intersected by useful rivers and springs which can irrigate it. And in those regions, too, in a certain valley, what is called balsam grows, from which they get a splendid revenue, since this plant is found nowhere else in the world, and the service it renders to doctors for making drugs is superlatively great."

Strabo, writing about the same time as Diodorus, describes the city and the people as they were at that date, and says that he derives his information from his friend Athenodorus, who is known as a Stoic philosopher and a friend and tutor of Augustus, and who had been born in Petra. Strabo's version is very different from that of Diodorus and (except in one matter) is entirely consistent with what the remains of Petra indicate to us as the life there in the first century B.C. He says:*

" The Nabataeans are temperate and industrious, so that a public penalty is imposed on the man who lessens his property, but to him that increases it honours, and, having few slaves, they are served for the most part by their relations, or by each other, or they serve themselves, so that the custom extends even to the Kings. They form ' messes ' of thirteen men each, and two singing-girls to each mess. The King in his great house holds many messes. No one drinks more than eleven cups in one and then another golden beaker. Thus the King is a democratic one, so that in addition to serving himself he sometimes even himself serves others. He often also submits his accounts to the people, and sometimes also the conduct of his life is inquired into. Their dwellings are extensive structures of stone, and their cities are unwalled on account of peace. Most of it abounds in fruit except the olive. They use oil made of sesame. Their sheep are white-haired, their oxen large: the country does not produce horses; camels render service instead of them. Even the Kings go out without tunics in girdles and slippers, but *they* go in purple. Some things are imported entirely, others not altogether, especially if they are produced in the country, as gold and silver and most of the spices. Copper and iron and, moreover, purple raiment, storax (a gum), costus (a root used as spice, like pepper), embossed work, paintings or drawings and moulded images, are not native productions. They think dead bodies no better than manure; as Heraclitus says, corpses are more to be thrown away than dungheaps. Wherefore they bury even their Kings beside their privies. They honour the sun, setting up an altar in the house, making libation on it daily, and using frankincense.

" First beyond Syria Nabataeans and Sabaeans occupy Arabia Felix, and often made inroads upon it before it became the possession of the Romans. But now both they and the Syrians are subject to the Romans. The capital of the Nabataeans is the so-called Petra. For it lies on ground in general even and level, but guarded all round by rock, outside precipitous and abrupt, but inside having abundant springs for drawing water and for gardening. Outside the circumference most of the country is desert, and especially that near Judaea.

" It is a three or four days' journey to Jericho and to Phoenicia five. Well it is ruled by one who is always of the royal family, and the King has as steward one of his companions, who is called ' Brother.' It has excellent laws. Athenodorus in truth, who was born among the Petraeans, a philosopher and a companion of mine, used to describe it in terms of wonder. He said that he found many Romans and many also of other foreign nations living among them; that he saw the strangers often contending (having lawsuits) both with one another and with the natives, but none of the natives bringing charges against each other, but keeping the peace perfectly among themselves.

" The expedition of the Romans against the Arabians that was lately made in our time, the leader of which was Aelius Gallus, teaches us many of the customs peculiar to the country. Augustus

* Strabo, Cap. 783, 784. Teubner Ed., pp. 1093-4.

F

Caesar sent him to gain some knowledge of these races and places, and of the Ethiopians, seeing that the Troglodyte country adjoining Egypt is a neighbour to these, and that the Arabian Gulf, which entirely separates the Arabians from the Troglodyte, is narrow. He determined to take these over or to subdue them, and it counted for something that they had the reputation from all time of being very wealthy, disposing of their spices and the most valuable marble for silver and gold, and spending nothing of what they received upon outsiders; for he hoped to enjoy them as rich friends or to conquer them as rich enemies. What induced him also was the hope he got from the Nabataeans who were friendly, and who promised to co-operate in all things."

Burton has a good deal to say about the origin of the Nabataeans in connection with his explorations in Midian.* He quotes Diodorus and Strabo—not omitting to add that both of them mention the disgraceful conduct of the Nabataeans by way of piracy in the Gulf of Akaba, which was presently forcibly stopped from Egypt. In discussing the name " Nabataean," he points out that it is often derived from a traditional descent from Nabajoth, the eldest son of Ismael. " Thus a so-called Scriptural name has evidently been given, after the fashion of the Jews, to a race much older than Abraham, Noah, and the Hebrew Adam himself." He discusses, and seems to be disposed provisionally to agree with, Quatremère in deriving their name rather from " Nabat or Nabata, the expression corresponding with what we popularly understand by Semitic." According to De Quatremère's investigations, the Nabataeans were really " the elder race of the great Aramaic family, the inhabitants of Babylon, before the Chaldeans, and the originators of . . . magic, natural and artificial; of astronomy . . . of medicine, and generally of the sciences which the world has attributed " to the Chaldeans. This origin is held to account for the contrast between the architecture of Petra— presumably one of their outposts—and all other Semitic architecture.

Very little is known about the religion of the Nabataeans as a nation, and even less, perhaps, about the religion of those of the nationality whom we may call particularly Petraeans, and who are responsible for the monuments of Petra. Strabo's opinion of their religiousness has already been quoted, and such information as can be gleaned from the Petraean inscriptions tends to confirm the idea that they were practically monotheistic. But we have no record of the qualities which they attributed to Dusares, or of the ritual of their worship in the days when the " holy places " of Petra were first organised. Sir George Adam Smith† mentions the names of a number of deities probably Nabataean, among which are Dusares and Allat. He considers Dusares as a Sun-God, which is also the statement made by Strabo. He also mentions the view that this name may mean Lord of the Shara, or " Mount Seir," the mountains of the Petraean district. Allat was " the Mother of the Gods." The Teima Stela (dated about the sixth century B.C.) of which a copy is in the British Museum, incidentally also gives several names as those of gods worshipped by the Nabataeans. But the only name which appears to be found at Petra, besides that of Dusares, is that of the female goddess Allat (identified by Herodotus as Aphrodite), which occurs only occasionally in graffiti.

From the great number of Triclinia which are to be found among the Petraean monuments it is clear that feasting must have been part of the ritual;—the feasts were doubtless funereal as well as religious. But in one case only (p. 58), so far as my observations go, is there a grave actually in a chamber which is a triclinium. It is quite possible, however, that, as for example, in the Triclinium opposite the Khazna, a recess in a side or back wall of a triclinium, or at a higher level, may have been used to carry a coffin, although not shaped in any special way like a grave.

* Burton, *The Gold Mines of Midian*, 1878.
† *Historical Georgraphy of the Holy Land*, 7th Edit., p. 628.

The city of Petra probably reached its greatest wealth and prosperity in the first and second centuries A.D. under the Romans. Whether the custom of carving dwellings or temples, tombs, or holy places out of the rocks continued to extend during this time is very doubtful. We know from the dated tombs at Madaïn Salih that the most complex and highly developed of the Petraean designs were already in existence before the commencement of our era. Up to this point there had been, during many centuries, a continuous development in Petraean architecture. With the introduction of the purely classical type of monument, probably at the beginning of the second century, the purely Nabataean development certainly ceased, whether or not monuments of Nabataean type continued to be built. And in the classical monuments there is no sign of any definite line of evolution. Moreover, in the whole of the remaining centuries during which the city lasted only some two dozen classical monuments appear to have been constructed. The Romans presumably preferred to build their monuments in the ordinary way within the walls of the city.

And so things continued, whilst the east-west traffic became gradually diverted to a more northerly route by Palmyra, and the north-south traffic probably took a line further east, something like the later Hajj route—the pilgrims' route from Damascus to Madina and very much the line of the present Hijaz Railway.

The Nabataean currency was replaced by Roman coinage about A.D. 67, but Petra appears for a long time afterwards to have held some special position in relation to the old Nabataean cult, for in the third century an annual festival in honour of Dusares and Allat is said to have been still held there. Karak (Al Crac) became eventually the capital of the whole district of Petra Deserti, and was the seat of a bishopric (or archbishopric), which was only extinguished by the Moslem power at the end of the seventh century. Whether the great Moslem invasion of that time found Petra already destroyed or not, which is doubtful, at any rate it left the district in that condition, the condition in which it has remained ever since. Its history becomes a blank for us until we hear of it again when the newly formed Kingdom of Jerusalem claimed *Oultre Jourdain* as a part of its fief. Baldwin I., immediately after his appointment as King (Christmas, 1100), made an expedition to the south and east of his domain, which is described by his Chaplain Fulcher. He was disappointed at not finding some reported spoil in the neighbourhood of Zoar. He then (with 150 knights and 500 footmen) " came into a mountain district, and from there, after five days' difficulties, came on the sixth day to a high mountain, where they found nothing but rain, ice, and snow, and thirty of the foot soldiers died." According to Fulcher (Chapter II., 5) the high mountain to which they came was that from which Moses brought the water by striking the rock, and at the same time was Mount Hor. (Fulcher says that the Arabs called the place Wadi Musa, which he reproduces as Vallis Moysi.) From this point the little army descended into a plain in which Baldwin found a prosperous village and good provision. He also heard that there was near by a town which could be easily taken, and where there would be plenty of booty. After four days' rest he started again on the fifth day and reached this town in the evening. Its inhabitants had taken to flight. He stopped there eight days, and on the tenth burnt the town and left it, returning by Zoar and Hebron to Jerusalem, which he reached in December.

Jabal Harun is not itself visible from the hollow of the Wadi Musa in which the city of Petra lay, and across which the water of Moses still flows (when there is any). But there is no place nearer the mountain to which the Arabs could possibly have given the name, so that we may reasonably infer that Baldwin's route from Jerusalem took him southward along the difficult country on either the west or east side of the Ghor, and that he then turned eastwards by the then well-known route round Jabal Harun on the south, which connects with the Roman route from

Aqaba through Sabra and directly northwards over Petra to al Baidha and thence in the direction of Shaubak.

I have quoted the story of Baldwin's raid in 1100 at so much length on account of its interest as being apparently the first glimpse we get of Petra, or of what once was Petra, after many centuries.

The doings of the Crusaders east of the Jordan—when *Oultre Jourdain* became a part of the Kingdom of Jerusalem—are very vaguely dealt with by the historians. It is clear that the main object of Baldwin I. and his successors was to get command of the South-North caravan route, with intent to harry and plunder. The forts at Le Crac (Karak) and Montreal (Shaubak) were either built or strengthened and garrisoned at this period, some time in the first half of the twelfth century. A fortress at Ouaira (Wu'aira) is also often mentioned, which the late writers connect with the Wadi Musa, but for which they cannot assign a definite site except that it was somewhere between Alji and Shaubak. Probably the difficulty of locating Wu'aira which the historians (being quite unfamiliar with the country) have found may have been largely due to an early mention of another fort called "Aswit," which was certainly also closely connected with the Wadi Musa. The authority in this case is a writer called Novairi, and it occurs in his detailed account of a visit of the Egyptian Sultan Bibars to Syria, *via* Petra, some years before his time. The details of the rocks and the caves which Novairi gives leave no doubt whatever that he is referring to Petra, and that the site of the city was then in much the same condition as that in which it still is. He says definitely that the Sultan *ascended* to some fort which was called Aswit, and which was close by stone steps leading to the grave of Aaron (Jabal Harun), and that afterwards he descended and continued his journey to Shaubak after examining the " villages of the children of Israel "—*i.e.*, the rock carvings. The existence of the Siq is alluded to, but apparently the ravine itself was not traversed. In the early part of the fourteenth century, therefore, there existed, or was believed to exist, on some elevation in or beside Petra, a " Castle " named Aswit. Novairi does not appear to make any suggestion that the castle had been built by the Crusaders. There is certainly no castle " close by " any steps or route leading to Jabal Harun. It might be conjectured that the curiosity of Bibars' followers would be more likely to be attracted by the fortification on Al Habis, probably close to their camp, than by the great fortress on the Obelisk ridge, an hour's journey away, and quite invisible. It might even be that the block monuments and the snake monument on the southern watershed, which were at any rate on the route to Jabal Harun, had got themselves translated into the fortress " built in a singular manner." (See Quatremère, *Mem. sur les Nabataeans*, 1835, and Carl Ritter.)

The only other reference to Al Aswit which I find is in Rey's *Colonies Franques en Syrie* (1883), where also Novairi is quoted as the authority. Rey adds that the castle is on the borders of the Siq, and that it lies between Mount Hor and Alji, and is a " little above " the theatre of Petra, not far from the building called Qasr Fi'run, and that it " was called Al Aswit when in 1116 it was occupied by King Baldwin I." For this last statement I can find no authority. A good many details are available as to Baldwin's Expedition of 1116, which he wound up by going south to Aqaba, but nowhere have I found in them any reference to Aswit. His primary object was to ensure the safety of his new fortress, which would naturally be Shaubak, " the first station east of the Jordan held by the Christians," which was taken possession of in 1114 or 1115. Rey adds that the castle of which he speaks is said to have communicated with Shaubak by a road passing through al Baidha.

The statement of Albert of Aix (the original is quoted by Musil) is that " Baldwin established a new garrison post in the course of eighteen days, so that he might the more effectually subdue the land of the Arabitae and that merchants might no longer be allowed to pass hither and thither across it without his permission, and that no ambuscades or forces of the enemy might suddenly make their appearance without showing themselves to the King's loyal subjects posted in the citadel." There is always a possibility that from the closeness of the dates quoted—1114-1116—there has been some confusion between Baldwin's doings at Shaubak and at Wu'aira.

About Wu'aira, although I have not found any more definite statement as to the year in which Baldwin garrisoned it, it certainly fell into the hands of " the enemy " again, and was recaptured by Baldwin III. in 1144, after an unsuccessful siege, only by a threat to cut down the olive trees which surrounded it, and which presumably constituted the chief means of livelihood for the inhabitants. This story is given in full by several writers. William of Tyre* says:

" The Turks, with the support and on the invitation of certain inhabitants of those regions, had occupied a certain strong place of ours, called the Vallis Moysi, in Syria-Sobal. Now the aforementioned town is hard by Aquae Contradictionis.† On learning, therefore, that the enemy were holding the aforesaid place, our lord the King sets out, and crossing with his expeditionary troops the famous valley where now the Dead Sea lies . . . they arrive at the point they aimed at. Now the inhabitants of that district had betaken themselves into the fort, taking for granted the strength of the place for the reason that it seemed impregnable. When our men, seeing the difficulty and insuperable strength of the place, after having spent some days in casting great stones, in many a discharge of arrows and other methods of offence, had found their labour useless, they had recourse to other tactics. The whole of that region was thickly planted with fertile olive trees—so thickly that they overshadowed the whole surface of the land, like very thick woods. It was resolved, therefore, to grub up these trees and burn them all." On this threat the fort capitulated.

The fort was finally lost by the Crusaders to Saladin, with the fortresses of Karak and Shaubak, in 1188-89, and never recovered.

The diligent historians of the nineteenth century were compelled to visualise the geography of Trans-Jordan from the very meagre accounts of many centuries earlier, given by travellers of whom few (except Fulcher) had ever seen the country. It is, therefore, not to be wondered at that they are somewhat vague as to details of places. On the whole, I have myself come to the conclusion that while there is no evidence that the Crusaders *built* any fort at the Wadi Musa, they garrisoned and probably enlarged the old fort at Wu'aira. As to the origin or history of the great fortifications on the Obelisk ridge, or the smaller buildings on al Habis, I have not found any evidence that would entitle an opinion to be expressed.

It seems clear that in the twelfth century no building in the city of Petra other than the Qasr Fi'run was standing; the site must then have been practically what it is to-day.

Then comes a sleep of five centuries, in which the rock-carved city disappeared into the region of legend, until an enterprising and courageous young Swiss explorer, on a pilgrimage to Mount Hor, found himself there, and recognised that the place he had come to must be the Petra of story, although circumstances allowed him only a single day there.

* *Historia Rerum XVII.*, Cap. 6, Anno 1144.
† I cannot identify these springs.

CHAPTER IV

THE MONUMENTS OF PETRA

I.—RECTILINEAR AND SPECIAL

OF the stone buildings which once formed the actual city of Petra, and probably covered an area of nearly a couple of square miles, there is still standing one single example only (Fig. 126), consisting of three walls of a Roman temple, dating possibly from the second or third century A.D., and therefore in no way whatever characteristic either of Petraean architecture or of the religion of Petra. The great series of rock-carved chambers and façades which have formed the chief interest of the place, and have been the object of so much curiosity and wonder and even admiration, have been very generally described by descriptively-minded visitors simply as *tombs*. They are, in fact—as the more exact examination of the last thirty years has shown—of very varied nature and purpose. They include many " holy places," sacella and others, with sacrificial arrangements—altars, basins, niches for offerings, shrines, symbolic (" idol ") blocks; triclinia for religious and funereal or other feasts; some imposing temples; many living chambers and others probably for trade purposes, as well as a great number of chambers forming places of sepulture.

Some day, it may be hoped, an investigating party (the work will require more than one person) may find time and opportunity to examine every accessible interior and determine, as far as may be possible, its original purpose. As one single word covering all these places, I have found it convenient to adopt the expression " monument," which, according to Dr. Johnson, means " anything by which the memory of persons or things is preserved."

It would be convenient, naturally, if we could deal with the monuments chronologically. But beyond the assumptions that monuments which distinctly show Greek influence in their design can hardly be dated before 300 B.C., and that the purely classical monuments (which happen to be those best known and most often illustrated, although they are relatively few in number) are almost certainly later than the end of the first century A.D.,* we have only considerations of a general nature to guide us in estimating the relative ages of the different types.

Such considerations cover the probable uses of the particular monuments, their comparative simplicity of design, and their condition as to weathering. To a certain extent, also, the positions of the monuments appear to afford some indication of their probable comparative age.

It is certain, however, that even in the latest time monuments of the earliest design may occasionally have been made, for the sake of economy or for other reasons. But these will remain exceptions, and do not interfere with the general development of design which took place steadily through the centuries.

Reminders of a time far before that of the rock-carvers are flint implements, of which any detailed examination of the surface would probably show many. Figs. 61 and 62 represent, more or less full size, two Palaeolithic tools found by Mr. Oscar Raphael in 1923. They were lying on the surface high up on the bank of the Nasara Wadi, near the point where it joins the main Wadi

---

* See Chapter VII.

Musa channel. They may be compared with the somewhat similar implements found in 1875 by Doughty near Ma'an, and illustrated in *Arabia Deserta.**

The much-weathered sandstone of Petra is absolutely riddled with natural caves, small and great, which can hardly fail to have been used as dwellings from the earliest times. For protection from the winter weather, as well as from enemies, the open front of the caves would, no doubt, be partly closed by a rough wall of stones. There are plenty of examples of this visible at the present day, due to temporary occupation by wandering Badawin.

Examples of open caves, which could be, and probably have been, used as dwelling-places, can be found almost at every turn in Petra. Fig. 63 represents a row of caves in the Siyagh close to what were doubtless important holy places.

An open cave at the north foot of Al Habis shows a plain, shallow niche in its back-wall which may obviously have held at some time a symbolic block. It would be very interesting to know whether the immense number of empty niches in the Petraean monuments were always empty— either mere prayer niches, or shelves for holding offerings—or whether the symbols which they once contained were intentionally thrown down and destroyed in some burst of Oriental iconoclastic fury.

The huge cave of Fig. 64 is one of these near the opening of the Siyagh gorge. Its three walls have been carefully squared, and are provided with a number of niches more suitable, apparently, for the storage of goods than for burials; and a shrine in the back-wall. There are no signs that this cave ever possessed a façade.

When the advantageous position of the place† led to more permanent and larger occupation, and more caves were discovered, the open-fronted dwelling would naturally be discarded for a cave only reached by a smaller opening which could be made into a doorway and so much more easily protected than an open front. A considerable number of monuments show recessed notches at the top of the doorways which are obviously intended to carry a wooden lintel. The doors themselves have, of course, disappeared, like all other woodwork, very long ago. In a few cases only the position of hinges is somewhat uncertainly visible, but no other traces remain. With the use of the same tools of metal which had made the doorway, the irregular cave could presently be squared out into a convenient living chamber, and of such there are a very large number at Petra, probably used simply as living places. The total number of these (apparently) cave dwellings has not been ascertained. Brünnow's list mentions more than sixty, the majority of them between the " Palace " and al Nasara. It is noticeable that the position of these chambers is such that they are often in close proximity to—if they do not actually form part of—a series of places of cult. The same is true of numerous (open) chambers in al Siyagh in relation to " holy places " there. The actual total is very much greater, however, than the number mentioned, as Brünnow's investigations were concerned chiefly with such later monuments as could be classified by their architectural features, and he omitted—of intention—the great number of *zerstörte Gräber* which he did not think it worth while to examine.

It cannot be said to be impossible that some of these simple chambers with doors may have been used as tombs, although they may contain nothing in the nature of an actual grave or its equivalent. The examination of a great number of monuments which have *certainly* been used as tombs has, however, shown us only two or three which have not had some kind of architectural façade. There are, of course, an immense number of architectural monuments which clearly have never been used as tombs, but if there are any considerable number of tomb-chambers which have not been architecturally treated I have not seen them.

* Vol. I., pp. 36-37, edition of 1921. † See Chapter I.

In Petra, however, and presumably enough contemporaneous with the rock dwellings, there are a very large number of simple rock-cut graves in the open. The majority of these are rebated round the edge, and no doubt all have been covered either by one large or several smaller stones. One in the outer Siq is shown in Fig. 65. Some of these graves are only a few feet deep, others as much as 10 or 12 feet. I found one (in an open part of the Farasa Wadi), with a little tree growing in it. The cover-stones have disappeared in almost every case. In many instances the apparent grave is a shaft communicating with a cave below, which is now quite open at the side, but which no doubt was once closed by solid protective masonry or timbering, so that bodies lowered into it could not be directly reached either by beasts or thieves.

A remarkable case of these shaft graves was discovered by Mr. Philby during our last visit. The badly-weathered monument having an arched top at al Nasara, shown at the extreme right of the row in Fig. 66 (No. 669 Br.), contains two chambers, each one reached by a shaft, open at the top, of dimensions suitable for lowering a body or a coffin. These shafts open straight into the chambers below, and can hardly have been intended for any other purpose than burial from above. It is inconceivable that the shafts should have been cut *after* the chambers had been excavated and the façade carved. Presumably the later architects had not looked at the top of their rock before they decided on carving the façade. When they finally excavated the chamber they must have been astonished to find two bodies already there.

The terrace at the top of the four monuments in Fig. 66 contains a number of simple rock-cut graves, besides the two shaft graves mentioned. The occurrence of such grouped graves is no doubt an indication, quite confirmed by the examination of the neighbouring monuments, that as a place for worship the Nasara district had some special sanctity. The left-hand monument (No. 666 Br.) in the figure contains a perfectly plain chamber; the two adjacent monuments (Nos. 667 and 668) have chambers with loculi, in which there may have been graves.

The open graves mostly occur in groups, and very often (as I have said) their occurrence seems to be due to the proximity of some place of cult.

The graves which are actually found within the chamber of a monument are of various kinds. Some are simple graves dug or quarried in the floor, of dimensions such as would hold a body or a coffin. Many are in the form of troughs (like mangers) carved in the back or side walls of the chamber, generally near the floor-level; some appear to be niches (or possibly troughs) somewhat high up in the walls. In a few cases (one of which is illustrated in Fig. 67) a corbelled recess in a back-wall is obviously devised so as to support a coffin.

On the east side of al Habis, at the foot of the ledge which circles round the rock and gives an easy access to the places of cult on its western side and on the top, a large cave which has been squared out into an open chamber contains in its walls two fairly large niches, and many small hollows, and may well have been a first " station " for the deposit of offerings by pilgrims or even to provide water for their fingers or for offerings. Just above this cave is another, which is now quite open and filled with some 4 feet of débris (Fig. 67), but which may at one time have had a carved front now destroyed by weather and stone falls. This cave contains on the upper part of its back-wall, above the débris, a recess about 10 feet wide and 2 feet deep corbelled as if to carry a coffin. Above the ledge for the coffin are carved geometrical grooves, of which I cannot suggest the significance. The walls where visible also contain a number of rectangular niches, each about 12 by 6 inches, as well as many smaller ones. The arrangement suggests that the chamber was the burial-place of someone distinguished by sanctity or otherwise, so that the body of the hero or saint might be approached by worshippers or pilgrims. Such a corbelled recess for carrying a coffin has only been noticed in one other case, which happens to be almost the only other instance found (see above) of a tomb without external architectural features. In this case, however, the chamber can only be approached by an elaborate flight of steps (p. 65) carved up the face of the rock, and leading apparently nowhere. Here also—but the coincidence may be accidental—the position of the tomb seems closely related to a remarkable " holy place," so that the chamber may well have been the burial-place of some specially distinguished person.

A type of monument, of which some examples, at any rate, must come very early in Petraean history, and of which the exact purpose still remains uncertain, is that to which Professor Musil gives the name " Sahrij."* These monuments take the shape of huge four-sided (detached) block towers some 20 to 30 feet in height. In all some twenty-six block towers have been counted by Brünnow, of which about half contain no chamber whatever. They occur chiefly in three districts— in the Bab al Siq, in the outer Siq, and in the white sandstone region near the southern watershed in the line of the main approach to Petra from the south and west.

The most notable Sahrij in the Bab al Siq is shown in Fig. 69 (No. 9 Br.). It carries no ornament beyond the vertical and horizontal grooves which give a suggestion of pilasters and cornices. It has neither door nor internal chamber. Fig. 190 (which also shows the remains of the barrage at the entrance to the Siq)† shows another block monument, entirely plain (No. 30 Br.), which is visible in the centre of the view. This block has both an internal chamber and a grave on its upper surface.

A group of block monuments (Br. 70-3), just at the western end of the outer Siq, is seen on the right-hand of Fig. 68. One of these monuments is split entirely in half. Fig. 70 is an isolated block on the opposite side of the valley to those of the last figure, and shows one of the instances in which the block is surmounted by crowstepped ramparts (in addition to having a normal Nabataean frieze) like those upon the bronze model of an Assyrian tower dated between 900 and 700 B.C., which is marked No. 91250 in the British Museum, and of which a photograph is given in Fig. 75.

It suggests itself that the block monuments with ramparts or a frieze may perhaps be later in date than those which are perfectly plain.

Fig. 71 shows one of the most notable of the block monuments—a Sahrij (No. 307 Br.) in the southern region. The same monument is seen, looked at from above, in Fig. 176, which shows that it apparently has a grave on its top surface. It has also an internal chamber, as to which see p. 70, while in form it is nearly a duplicate of the Sahrij in the Bab al Siq (Fig. 69). It has a crowstep frieze on one side at least, possibly a decoration added later. Fig. 72 shows, on the right-hand slope, a large plain block (Br. 303), which has a door and internal chamber.

The small chambers in these monuments, where they exist, were probably for burials; they appear too small for dwellings. But in the numerous cases where no sepulchral use was intended or possible, it may have been that the towers were looked at simply as a glorified version of the block symbol of Dusares, used by their constructors to represent the deity they worshipped, or of the altar used in his worship.

---

* The Arabic word *Sahrij* (plural *Saharij*) is derived or corrupted from the Mesopotamian dialectic form (*Chariz*) of the Persian *Kariz* denoting a subterranean water-channel and, by a natural extension of meaning, a cistern or reservoir whether subterranean or not. In Central Arabia such channels are called *Saqi* or *Kharaz* (apparently another form of *Kariz*); at Jidda in the Hijaz the term *Sahrij* is used to denote subterranean cisterns filled by torrent water from *Wadis* leading down to them; and at Aden the same term is applied to the famous open tanks in the " Crater." The block monuments of Petra have, of course, nothing to do with the water-supply, but are sufficiently like tanks to be called *Sahrij* by the Arabs, particularly when they are situated like those in the Bab al Siq area on the brink of the Wadi Musa.

† See also p. 73.

Among the oldest monuments which were, or may have been, used as tombs would certainly appear to be those—not very numerous—of which examples are given in Figs. 73, 74, 79, and 81. In these cases the only decoration consists of straight lines, either raised or hollowed out in grooves. Comparison with any of the " false doorway " reliefs in the British Museum, or (as an elaborate example) the sarcophagus of Khufu-Ankh (Fig. 76), seems to indicate an Egyptian origin for this very formal rectilinear ornament.

Perhaps it would be more to the point to note the resemblance between these " rectilinear " façades and the conventional thrones on a Babylonian " boundary stone " of a date about 1100 B.C.*

It is very possible that these " rectilinear " monuments may be altogether older than the Nabataean possession of Petra. On the other hand, the suggestion occurs naturally that the increased complexity of the later monuments came about *pari passu* with an improvement and extension in the methods and tools available for rock-carving.

The monuments with rectilinear carving do not occur in any one part of Petra, but are found— I have said they are comparatively few in number—in widely separated positions.

The small monument in Fig. 74 is in one corner of the garden court (Fig. 138) behind al Habis. It is, however, apparently much older than the other principal monument in the court, for its door opening is about 6 feet above the floor-level of the court, which is now reached by a short downward flight of cross-steps so placed as now to cut off the monument altogether. The chamber is so filled with débris that it is not possible to say whether it contains any grave or not. The front contains both raised and grooved lines, all perfectly straight.

The two small tombs in Fig. 73 (Br. Nos. 450-451) are close to the " Lion " monument at the foot of the Wadi al Dair. Both these are graves, and actually still contained bones in 1923 and 1924. The decoration of the left-hand tomb is nearly the only one of its kind. The upper bar is angled as if it were the top of a flat pediment. There are no grooves, but only spaces between horizontal ridges. The right-hand tomb has one straight bar only above the doorway, the latter having been cut or broken open sideways. The monument is flanked by two very elementary pilasters of which the capitals have been broken away, if they ever existed. Across the top there appears to have been a straight flat moulding.

The monument in Fig. 79 (probably Br. 320), which has a certain resemblance to the last, is in the Wadi Thughra, half-way up to the southern graves. Here the flat pilasters are applied to the doorway as well as to the sides of the front wall. The top has gone altogether. There were no signs of burial in the chamber, which was broken through on one side. The lightly carved obelisk on the right-hand side of the door perhaps bears witness to the piety of the owner.

The monument in Fig. 82 is one of the many choked up graves in the lowest slope of the Obelisk ridge in the outer Siq, south of the theatre. It is one of the very few instances of the use of the mere shape of a pediment as a piece of decoration, as mentioned above. If the upper part of the façade has not been weathered or broken away, this is the only case which has been noticed in which a single crowstep frieze has been finished with a straight moulding above it. In any case this feature occurs extremely seldom in Petra, although there are instances of it at Madaïn Salih.

Fig. 81 is a good example of an extremely weather-beaten tomb with a straight groove and with lintel notches, on the west side of the Obelisk ridge. The doorway of a storehouse in the outer Siq (Fig. 83), the interior of which is shown in Fig. 204, is another case of the use of the pedimental form. Here it will be noticed that in the base of the triangle a piece of stone is fixed (it was too tightly jammed to be knocked out) which may have been a part of a complete filling of the whole triangle

* Jastrow, *Civilisation of Babylonia*, p. 417, Plate LXXII.

with separate—possibly decorative—material. Several other cases will be mentioned in which grooves are still wholly or partly filled up in this way. There appear to be no means of saying whether or not the practice was usual, or whether the mere straight line in itself had some esoteric meaning unknown to us. Fig. 84 shows another very similar interior.

The front of the monument in Fig. 98 (near Br. 453 in the Wadi al Dair) is simpler in its design. It is one of those which show also the notches at the top of the cut doorway for a wooden lintel. The two vertical side openings are probably light holes cut at some date by Badawin occupants. The niche on the left of the doorway may either have been simply a shelf for small offerings, or may have held a block image. It contains two (rebated) niche graves.

A monument for which no obvious purpose suggests itself and which does not seem hitherto to have been noticed is shown in Fig. 85. It consists of a wall perhaps 30 feet high facing a large cleared level space between rough side-walls, and looking like a gigantic fives court. On the face of the wall are cut out six shallow vertical niches (apparently unfinished) each about 6 feet high and 3 or 4 feet broad. Above them are four large holes, each a foot square and of some depth. These last may well have been used in the construction of a timber roof. The whole wall is so much weathered that this monument has certainly every appearance of great age. The monument forms a retaining wall at the southern end of the great clearing which forms the " garden " (Fig. 149) of the Temple (Fig. 106) in Al Ma'aisara. In Fig. 153 it is seen against the skyline in the middle of the picture. It is reached by a flight of steps (hidden behind the large monument with the cornice) as well as by a deep artificial couloir seen (from the level of the top of the monument) in Fig. 154. The garden itself is reached by the rough slope in Fig. 153, the steps on which are too much worn to be visible. The garden " Temple " is obviously connected with the arrangement of a " holy place " above it reached by many steps (see p. 66).

The shallow rectangular niches of the wall are somewhat reminiscent of the rock-wall at al Khuraiba (El Khreyby) discovered by Doughty,* where, beside a number of wall graves, were shallow niches containing images of monsters in high-relief. The Petra niches, however, are very much larger than those described by Doughty. The latter are excellently illustrated in Jaussen's photographs.†

Only two other monuments in Petra have been noticed as containing any number of similar large high shallow niches. One is a three three-sided court immediately above a large tank or reservoir cut out of the hillside above the Temple at the entrance of the Farasa Wadi on its north-east side. This court is shown in Fig. 171. It has five flat niches along one side, four in the back-wall and three in the other side, on which, however, room is left for two more niches, which would make the two sides symmetrical, and the whole number of niches fifteen. A ledge along each wall, above the niches, is just at the level of the springing of the arch seen on the back-wall, and suggests that the whole court has been arched over, in which case its date would probably be Roman. (Brünnow gives a sketch-plan in Fig. 309.) The second is the large classical tomb of Fig. 124 (Br. No. 228) described later on.

In the Bab al Siq are two other monuments, which in external appearance, and to a great extent in internal arrangement also, are unique in Petra. One of them is known as al Khan (Br. No. 4), and is the first monument in the district to become visible to anyone approaching from Alji, or coming down from Ras al Khaur, in the direction of the Siq. Its position makes it probable that al Khan had a purpose in connection with religious rites, and it is fully described later on in the

---

* *Arabia Deserta*, Vol. I., Chap. VI., p. 159.
† *Mission Archéologique en Arabie*, Jaussen and Savignac, *Atlas*, Pts. xxi. and xxiii.

chapter dealing with Cult. Some of the earlier observers have said that the front of Al Khan was flanked by two gigantic lions, which later visitors have been unable to discover. In March last, when descending from Alji on the opposite side of the valley, I noticed that the natural shaping of two projecting rocks in front gave them a rough resemblance to animals' heads, and this may have been at the bottom of the statement.

The second unique monument (Br. No. 35) lies 700 or 800 yards nearer the Siq and on the opposite side of the Wadi Musa. It is the upper part of what looks like a double monument in Fig. 86. The lower part is probably of later date, and will be described in its proper place among the classical monuments (p. 52). The upper monument contains an internal chamber about 20 feet by 16 feet, with two graves on each side of it and a single grave in the back-wall. The place of the usual carved façade is taken by four large obelisks, quite detached from the front wall of the chamber, each standing on a square block base, and devoid of any ornament. Although this is the only case in Petra of such a use of obelisks, the obelisk outline occurs over and over again in graffiti (such as is seen in Fig. 79) in company with inscriptions (see p. 76), recording the names of the engravers and often enough the name of the deity in whose honour and for whose remembrance they have been drawn. A natural inference from the occurrence of these four obelisks (originally about 23 feet in height) would be that their origin was Egyptian. This, with the plain simplicity of the whole monument, suggests that it is of very early date. But, on the other hand, the door between the two middle obelisks has an architrave of ordinary classical type bearing a line of triglyphs. Higher up above this door is a rectangular niche similarly decorated, and filled with a statue. In the chamber, also, the opening of the central niche grave is flanked by pilasters and surmounted by a flat moulded arch, a feature somewhat rare in Petra, and certainly pointing to a fairly late date. With these contradictory features, the age of the monument must be left unguessed. The monument below it is purely classical—and not Nabataean—in its architecture, and from its florid design would naturally be placed somewhat late in the classical period. And the fact that the two monuments are by no means exactly in line one above the other seems a fairly certain indication that they were not constructed at the same time, and that they are entirely without original connection. The Obelisk monument clearly was the first made (whatever the difference in date may be), for the façade of the lower monument has had to be flattened down in a very ungainly fashion because there was no room to carry it higher. David Roberts' drawing of this double monument forms a curious exception to his general great accuracy. He has obviously made sketches on the spot, and finished them later on when he had quite forgotten the relative positions of the two façades, which he places at some distance apart in a much more picturesque relation to each other, and close to a distant Sahrij.

II.—MONUMENTS OF ASSYRIAN TYPE

Apart from the monuments discussed in the last chapter, and those others which appear to be more or less directly connected with religious cult, the immense majority of the Petraean rock-fronts may be classed shortly as being either Nabataean or classical. Brünnow's enumeration makes the total of these about 520. But, as mentioned above, there are literally hundreds more of a Nabataean type which, on account of their physical condition, he did not think it worth to include in his list.

As none of these *zerstörte Gräber* are classical in type, the five-and-twenty classical monuments scheduled by Brünnow, with a few others in al Baidha and al Barid which he was unable to examine, represent really the whole number of that type out of the many hundreds of monuments in Petra. It is of some importance that this should be understood, as the many hasty visitors to Petra who have published their reminiscences seem to have been so impressed by the glory of the Khazna in its dark ravine and the magnificence of the Dair on its noble summit, or of the grand façade of the " Palace," that for them these classical or quasi-classical monuments have represented Petra, although in fact the really characteristic Petraean rock-carving was something entirely different, and something which had commenced five or six centuries before any of the classical monuments existed, and which, moreover, practically died when they were born.

In speaking of monuments in this connection it has to be remembered that it is only their external appearance—their façades*—which are at this stage specially dealt with or differentiated. *Internally* they are all alike in containing a rectangular chamber or chambers, frequently with wall niches, sometimes with a shrine (occasionally decorated), and often having raised benches on three sides, as in a triclinium. *Externally* the monuments, considered as a whole, show a continuous development from plainness and simplicity to ornateness and complexity of design. Internally no such development is traceable.

Among the monuments which are of pre-classical date, and which therefore must have been carved by the Nabataean people, or at any rate in Nabataean times, there are about thirty of a type totally different from the rest, which do not fall in any way into the line of development. These monuments have their upper parts in the form of a half-round arch, the tympanum of which often contains some decoration. It has been suggested that their design is Syrian in origin. As their relative number and importance in Petra is very small, they will be left out of account in dealing generally with the Nabataean monuments; Fig. 87 is a typical example of a pair of them. The absence of the Nabataean capital (see p. 58) in these tombs is noteworthy. The plain angled capital of Fig. 87 occurs frequently at Madaïn Salih, but in no other places at Petra.

The characteristic Nabataean monuments, through all their modifications, contain in some form a feature which appears clearly to be borrowed from Assyrian architecture, of which Figs. 75, 77 and 78 are examples from the British Museum. Fig. 77 is a part of panel 45 of the great relief of the lion hunt of Assur-bani-pal. Fig. 78 is from a small bronze model of a house-front. The latter shows also a geometrical decoration in equilateral triangles which has remained in use even to the present day in various places in Trans-Jordan. There is an example in a fortified house in the principal street in Ma'an, and Jaussen has illustrated several examples of different ages in the neighbourhood of Madaïn Salih. The bronze tower of Fig. 75 shows the same thing.

It is interesting to note that the Assyrian crowstep frieze has also been used along the top of Ibn Saud's great palace at Riyadh, illustrated by Mr. Philby in his *Heart of Arabia*, Vol. I., p. 68. The feature referred to is the use, purely for purposes of decoration, of what resemble crowstep gables, either (*a*) in one or two horizontal lines as a sort of frieze, or sometimes forming ramparts, or (*b*) in the shape of two large (sometimes gigantic) separated half-gables. In a recent paper I have called only the (*a*) type *Assyrian*, and proposed the name *Egyptian* for the (*b*) type, on account of the fact that in that type there is always used a cornice like an Egyptian " cavetto." As, however, both types make use of an essentially Assyrian feature it is perhaps less misleading to call the (*b*) type by another name, a matter which is discussed later on.

Out of all the Nabataean monuments—in other words, out of the great bulk of the monuments in Petra—considerably more than one-half belong to the (*a*) type, which may be called shortly the Assyrian type. Groups of these monuments† are shown in Figs. 89 to 91. These photographs

---

* Doughty calls them " frontispieces."

† Brünnow calls these monuments by the convenient, but not strictly accurate, name of *Pylons*.

show examples of Assyrian façades both with single and double rows of crowsteps. Fig. 88 shows more clearly the details of a single monument. Distinctive details, which are repeated without change in all the hundreds of similar monuments, are: (1) That the line of crowsteps subdivides into units each consisting of two half-gables, and not into units of complete gables, each end of the line being thus a half gable;—among the many cases of crowsteps in the Assyrian reliefs at the British Museum I have only found a single one which is an exception to this; (2) that there are always four steps in each gable (the Assyrian reliefs have *three*); and (3) that there is a straight bar moulding above and below the lower frieze where there are two lines of gables, but only below, and not above, the upper or a single frieze. The number of semi-gables in a row is not constant, but varies with the breadth of the monument.

The monuments of this simple Assyrian type are distributed widely over Petra, but they are most numerous on both sides of the outer Siq. Fig. 89 shows a part of the immense group of monuments (Nos. 105-119 Br., etc.) on the west side of the outer Siq and adjoining the theatre, a portion of the latter being visible on the right of the photograph. A great fall of rock or débris has at some time overwhelmed many of these monuments, of which there have been apparently three, if not four, rows, one above the other. The lowest row, or rows, have been practically wiped out. Fig. 91 shows other monuments (Nos. 101-134 Br.) of the same group, further south. One of these (No. 103 Br.) is shown by itself in Fig. 88. This is a large tomb with a double row of crow-steps. It is approached by three broad steps.

Fig. 90* is a part of an equally large group of Assyrian type monuments covering the east side of the outer Siq. The tall monument (No. 780 Br.), which is so rough near the bottom that it may never have been finished, contains only a perfectly plain low chamber. The smaller monument (No. 781 Br.) next to it in a recess has a chamber having eight vertical niches, or loculi, on each side of a large niche, with an architrave opening into a second chamber which contains a trough grave. It would seem to be eminently possible, from what we know of primitive civilisation, that the loculi were occupied as dwelling-places of the family whose chief member was buried beside them. The next monument beyond this one (not visible in the photograph) has also at the back of the chamber an alcove (with an arched back) containing a trough grave and having a deep idol niche beside it.

Although there are many parts of Petra in which the ground may be said without much exaggeration to be "covered" with monuments, there is no other district where quite so many are crowded into so small a space as in what I have called the outer Siq. It has been plausibly suggested that the reason for this may have been the immediate neighbourhood of the great ridge on which the pair of obelisks (Fig. 164) suggest the existence of worship in very early times, continued for many centuries doubtless in the elaborate place of sacrifice which has so often been illustrated.† The desire of Jews and Muhammadans to be buried close to the site of the Temple or the Haram al Sharif at Jerusalem has similarly led to the covering of the slopes of the Mount of Olives with thousands of graves—and burials there still continue.

Fig. 92 (which covers Nos. 361-381 Br., etc.) is a part of the east wall of al Biyara (behind the rock of al Habis) on the side of Petra opposite to the Siq, and shows also the condition of the lower and more ancient monuments which Brünnow classified (only too accurately) as *zerstörte Gräber* and only a few of which are included in his lists. Fig. 93—a part of the west wall of the Wadi al Dair (Nos. 438-440 Br.), north of the Wadi Musa, shows just as distinctly the extent to which monu-

---

* At the foot of this photograph, in the right-hand corner, is the triple cave, with steps to an altar place higher up, of Fig. No. 162.

† See Chapter IV., v., and Figs. 163 and 164.

ments have been destroyed or rendered unrecognisable by the effects of time and weather, and Fig. 66 gives a very picturesque illustration of the same thing at al Nasara (Nos. 666 to 669 Br.).*

The monuments of Assyrian type on al Ma'aisara are also very numerous (Fig. 94, Nos. 522-539 Br.), although more scattered than in the Outer Siq.

Fig. 95 (No. 313 Br.) is a double-storey tomb of the Assyrian type. It is in the Wadi Thughra, practically on the western wall of al Barra, and close to the region of the monuments in the white sandstone of the Southern Watershed. The chamber is unusually large—36 feet wide by 24 feet deep—containing a complicated system of niches of which several certainly appear to be graves. There are two longitudinal openings in the front wall beside the door, made either for light or ventilation, possibly long after the monument had ceased to contain any corpses.

It is worth while noticing that although the outer Siq is crowded with Nabataean monuments both of the earliest and later "Assyrian" types, there appear to be only three normal Nabataean façades in the whole of the monuments of the Bab al Siq—*i.e.*, beyond the eastern end of the Siq.

By way of further ornamentation than the friezes, the majority of the Assyrian monuments have either nothing whatever or else—as in most of those in the groups photographed—simply a straight groove over the door. It is probable, although by no means certain, as has already been mentioned, that these grooves may have been originally filled by the insertion of a separate bar of a different stone, or even of wood. This may even, of course, have carried on it an inscription giving some indication of ownership, which otherwise would appear to have been entirely wanting. The straight line groove is in itself very reminiscent, as has been pointed out above, of the early Egyptian doorways. It may possibly have had some esoteric meaning not now intelligible to us. Altogether only about a dozen monuments of this class have even a straight architrave carved over the door, while three (of which one is seen in Fig. 89) have a quasi-classical pediment.

III.—MONUMENTS OF CORNICED TYPE

The Nabataean monuments which are not described in the last chapter have a feature in common which led me to suggest the name "Egyptian" as suitable for the whole of them. All of them, excepting only two or three freaks, carry a heavy quadrantal cornice, like the Egyptian *cavetto*. All of them also, however, carry—above the cornice (sometimes above a second cornice)—crowsteps of a type having clearly an Assyrian origin. These monuments therefore appear still to owe their most notable feature to Assyrian suggestion, and the use of the name "Egyptian" may be considered misleading. The line or lines of small crowstep "gables" are here replaced by two very large half-gables, covering the whole of the upper part of the monument above the cornice, not unfrequently 8 feet, or even more, in height.

I propose to call this type of decorated Nabataean monument "corniced," which suggests no misleading connotation. These corniced monuments, like those of the Assyrian type, are distributed over the whole area of Petra. The groups of Assyrian monuments in the outer Siq and behind al Habis (Figs. 89 to 91, etc.) show a few of them. There are many more, however, in the Wadis and ridges of Al Ma'aisara (Fig. 94), and at al Nasara, as well as along the western wall of the Obelisk ridge up to the Farasa and Numair Wadis.

In its simplest form† there is no ornament or decoration at all on the façade beyond the common straight groove over the doorway. Fig. 96 is an example on slopes south of al Nasara not far from Br. No. 659, the small chamber in which contains two loculi, probably for graves.

These simple corniced monuments so much resemble an altar in shape and design as to suggest

---

* See p. 40 *ante.*
† Quite suitably called *Stufengrab* by Brünnow.

that this resemblance may be the origin of their special form. In the British Museum, among the Assyrian reliefs (Assyrian Basement, panel 92), is one showing (*inter alia*) an altar with crowstepped horns and with a straight moulding below the horns in the position of the cornice on the monuments. But it must be said that this suggested origin is not strengthened by the fact that the very many graffiti of altars scratched on the Petraean rocks invariably (at least I have seen no exception) show plain—straight or convex—horns not stepped in any way, if they show any horns at all. And the stepped altar horns in panel 92 at the British Museum do not represent a form common there.

Fig. 97 shows a tomb behind al Habis, a small chamber which contains graves, and which lies above the Garden Court, and must be a very early example of " decoration," both at the sides of the face and round the doorway. The capitals of the would-be pilasters have clearly been originally of the Nabataean type. The holes on the sides of the door were probably cut through the thin front wall as air-holes when the chamber was used as a habitation.

Fig. 80 has, on the right, the tomb (of this type) in the Garden Court already referred to (see Fig. 138). No more than traces of pilasters are left, and the underside of the cornice seems to be weathered away into a series of brackets. The chamber contains a single trough grave. The door on the left opens into a plain chamber only, of which there are two more round the Court. Fig. 101 is a corniced tomb in a very similar condition, with an idol niche to the left of the door. The apparently much older monument of Fig. 74 mentioned in the last chapter is at the diagonally opposite corner of the Court, but at a much higher level.

Only about one-fifth of about 200 corniced monuments are quite plain-fronted and have perfectly simple doorways.

The first step in the way of decoration, after the use of pilasters, may have been the doubling of the cornice, so as to make an " attic " below the crowsteps. Later on the attic was filled with a " second order," generally in the shape of reproductions of the capitals of the columns or pilasters below. The doorways became elaborately classical in design, and sometimes two extra pilasters were added to the façade.

Fig. 99, a view of the upper part of the outer Siq (east wall), taken looking down from above, shows several notable monuments of the more decorated corniced type. The large monument on the left hand (No. 808 Br.) is one in which Mr. Gray Hill found in 1896* a stone with a Nabataean inscription, which he states must have been taken out of a grave in a loculus which had apparently been recently opened. The inscription mentions the brother of a Queen of the Nabataeans, of a date corresponding to about A.D. 71. The stone afterwards disappeared, but not before the inscription had been deciphered. There is no reason to doubt Mr. Gray Hill's statement as to the place from which it came. According to his examination the grave must have been covered with about 2 feet of " not very hard " concrete. The next monument to the right (over a line of smaller and much weathered tombs) is No. 813 Br., with a façade having a similar classical doorway and a plain attic between two cornices. Of the interior of this I have no note. Beyond it, near the foot of the photograph, and almost in the centre, are two monuments of which one (on left) hides much of the second, which is in a deep recess. The first is the Block Monument of Fig. 70 (824 Br.). The second (Fig. 100, No. 825 Br.), is one which is quite unique in its internal arrangement. It contains a large chamber, on the floor of which are fourteen graves, very irregularly disposed. In the back-wall is a large niche, partly arched, which contains three more graves. On one side-wall a group of five obelisks has been scratched, and a single obelisk on the other wall. This seems the only case in which obelisks are directly connected with graves. On the bases of two of the

* See *Q.S.*, 1897, p.136.

obelisks are scratched short inscriptions naming a son and a grandson of one Iakum, but no indication as to their date.

It is singular, and very notable, that in the Petraean monuments the large double crowsteps are always accompanied by the heavy cornice, and the cornice by the double crowsteps. There are practically no cases where the cornice is surmounted by the original line of small crowsteps. Indeed, the only exception which I have noticed is in the case of an unfinished Block Monument in the Outer Siq, standing quite isolated on its four sides, having two full cornices, the upper one carrying a row of five small crowstep gables forming ramparts. This monument (No. 70 Br.) has an elaborately decorated classical doorway, which, however, has never been opened out, and pilasters with Nabataean capitals, with low-relief carving, as in the Lion Monument (see p. 57). There seems to have been some very rigid architectural law or convention in Petra which absolutely prevented any mixture of the two types. A similar rigid convention* seems to have prevented the use of a straight moulding above an upper line of crowsteps in the Assyrian type of monuments. In Madaïn Salih, in the first century A.D., the architects were either much less strict or ignorant of the rigid rules of those whom they were imitating, for there are several cases of mixture of designs which would not apparently have been tolerated in Petra.†

At a later stage the doorway as well as the main front received its own decoration of classical pilasters and architraves, and finally an attic was added between two cornices. In the monument of Fig. 101 there appear originally to have been side pilasters, which, however, are now only doubtfully recognisable. On the left of the doorway is a niche for offerings, or once containing a block. Fig. 102, a monument in al Nasara (No. 651 Br.), shows a very elaborate doorway and a perfectly plain attic, half the crowsteps being broken off. In the huge monument in the outer Siq (Fig. 103, No. 67 Br.), a second chamber has been excavated, with a rather elaborate doorway, in the space between the two ranges of steps. The latter appear to be surmounted by another (a third) cornice. The local story or legend is that this upper chamber was occupied by a noted robber or outlaw, who reached it by jumping over the space on the right of the monument, and so evaded his enemies.

In the Turkamaniya tomb (Fig. 104, No. 633 Br.) the attic is much elaborated, and is filled with a second order consisting of duplicated upper parts and capitals of the columns below, which in this case are four in number. On the flat space between the two middle columns is a long Nabataean inscription, the only one of its kind,‡ which shows that the monument was a burying-place. It contains two chambers, one opening out of the other. The outer and larger is about 36 feet square (the dimensions in Brünnow's sketch are too small), with an inner doorway, 8 feet wide and round topped, leading into a second chamber of equal width with the first but only about 20 feet deep. In the partition wall over the passage between the two rooms is a recess about 6 feet deep, which appears designed to contain two bodies or coffins side by side. At the back of the second chamber is a recess in which is a horizontal niche of dimensions proper to hold a single body or coffin.

One of the most beautiful of the Petraean decorated monuments (Fig. 105, No. 770 Br.) is under the east wall of al Khubdha, close to the Palace and Corinthian Monument.§ Its beauty, however, depends chiefly on its colours and not on its form, and these cannot, of course, appear in the photograph. The façade of this monument is of the same type as that of the Turkamaniya tomb, with four pilasters and an attic in which the capitals are repeated. It has not, however, the duplicate lower cornice, but it has a second chamber above the principal one.

Two examples of the most ornate type of decorated corniced monuments, which are in a somewhat better state of preservation, are those of Figs. 106 and 107. Neither appear to be tombs; one

* See p. 46.   † See Chapter VII.   ‡ See Chapter VI.   § See p. 55.

H

is arranged internally as a triclinium, and both are fronted by large cleared spaces. The monument of Fig. 106 (No. 559 Br.) on al Ma'aisara is at the head of the great Garden Court described in p. 66. It is in direct communication, by elaborate steps leading upwards, with a stibadium (Fig. 150) and various water-carrying arrangements which appear to belong to a place where some kind of religious ceremonies were performed.

Fig. 107 appears to be a large triclinium. It is in the Nasara region, standing immediately above a hollow way which forms part of an ancient route from Petra northwards. In this case the attic is so shallow as to allow just depth only for the copied capitals. Between them is placed a group of four shields and two Medusa heads.

Fig. 108 (Nos. 195, 196 Br.) is a good illustration of the wonderful way in which the " ravages of time " have added to the picturesqueness of the Petraean monuments. On the left is a corniced and decorated monument so worn that it is hardly possible to say whether it had originally two or four pilasters in front, or whether the doorway had any decoration. The two splendid buttresses which enclose the next monument do not appear to owe anything to the hands of man. The organ-pipe fluting higher up must also be entirely natural—there are many instances of it in Petra. (In the much older (Carboniferous) sandstone near Dawlish and Teignmouth can be seen in the cliffs examples of the " pot-holes " at Petra which look so much like water-worn rocks, and also examples (although not so well marked) of the organ-pipe weathering.) An upper chamber has here been cut out (as in Fig. 103) between the feet of the crowsteps. On the ground at the right of the photograph is seen the upper part of a large façade which has split off the cliff and fallen down. The group in Fig. 109 lies on the west wall of the Obelisk ridge not far from the opening of the Wadi Farasa.

Of interest in connection with the corniced monuments are Figs. 109, 110, and 115, belonging to entirely different districts in Petra. Fig. 109 shows a slice of the west wall of the Obelisk ridge, where there are three, or sometimes four, tiers of monuments, one over the other. All those shown in the figure are of corniced type, mostly not " decorated "—in the neighbourhood of No. 197 Br.

Fig. 110 represents a very conspicuous line of four decorated corniced monuments on the east side of Wadi Ma'aisarat al Westani. All four have classical doorways, pilasters, and double cornices with an attic. For some unknown reason, but probably owing to unsoundness in the rock, the front of the second monument of the group, which apparently had an upper chamber, has fallen entirely away. The right-hand monument in the photograph (No. 524 Br.) has a large chamber containing no visible graves but three niches only, presumably for idols.

Fig. 115 is on the north side of the northern block in al Nasara, the monuments being apparently Nos. 675 and 676 Br. Both are of the decorated type, and No. 676 at least has a double cornice. The last named has a large chamber with five loculi on each side, and as many in the back-wall, besides four small niches about 15 feet up on the back-wall, covered in with masonry blocks which have been disturbed. No. 675 Br. has three shallow recesses, each about 9 feet by 5 feet, separated by pilasters, on the back-wall. On the right-hand wall is a large recess 3 feet from the ground.

A very notable feature in the Nabataean monuments of the " decorated " type is the constancy in the design of the capitals of the pilasters or the columns. This matter will be illustrated in the following chapter.

It may well be supposed that the reign of King Aretas III., who has been called the " Philhellene," from 80 to 65 B.C., was favourable to the adoption of Greco-Roman decoration in the Nabataean monuments, and that many of the more decorative corniced monuments date from about this period.

IV.—MONUMENTS OF CLASSICAL TYPE

The best known and most often illustrated class of monuments in Petra is represented by a far smaller number of monuments than the types described in the preceding chapters. This class may fairly be described as of " classical " type. It discards entirely the most characteristic feature of the Nabataean monuments, the use of " crowstep " decoration in some form. It discards also the cornice or cavetto, which had probably been used in the more developed Petraean monuments for at least two centuries before any of the classical type came into existence. The fact that no single monument of the type exists at Madaïn Salih, where during the first century A.D. nearly every one of the other Nabataean varieties were copied (and dated), affords a fair presumption that there were no classical monuments at Petra before, at the earliest, the very end of that century. We may reasonably infer that the classical monuments came into existence after the taking over of the Nabataean kingdom by Trajan in A.D. 106.

In the course of their development the Nabataean architects had, by that time, assimilated many Greco-Roman ideas which may conveniently be included generally under the one title of classical. These had been applied, however, chiefly to the enrichment of the doorways—(see, for example, Figs. 106 and 107)—rather than to the design of the façades as a whole. In what I have called the classical type of monument the whole façade is redesigned. Columns or engaged pilasters remain, as in the later monuments of the corniced type—their capitals, oddly enough, still of the Nabataean design—but the crowsteps, and with them the cornice of the more developed Nabataean type, disappear entirely. All these features are replaced by a purely classical pediment, familiar no doubt to the Romans, who may have become the chief inhabitants of the city.

The statement is made by Miss Martineau, and one or two other of the older explorers, that the capitals of the pilasters were not carved out of the solid, but made separately, and pinned on by metal pins. It is possible that this may have been the case here and there, but certainly only exceptionally. There are innumerable instances in which the capitals are weathered and broken in such fashion as shows clearly that they are parts of the living rock, like the columns themselves.

In the details of the pediments there are very considerable variations, but I do not see anything indicating a progressive development of orthodox western methods, such as clearly took place with the Nabataean designs.

The classical monuments, somewhere about twenty-five in number, in Petra itself, are mostly to be found on the eastern side of the city. There are several more in al Baidha (see Chapter I., vii.). There is a single one only (Fig. 86) (already mentioned) in the Bab al Siq. Within the Siq itself, in a cross opening near its western end, stands the Khazna Fir'un, which from its picturesque and unexpected appearance in the ravine (Fig. 111), as well as from its striking form, has become the best known and the most discussed of all the Petraean monuments. On the east side of the outer Siq, immediately facing the theatre, is a notable temple (Fig. 116) surmounted by a large urn, which has given it the name of the " Urn-tomb," although it does not appear to be in any way connected with sepulture. In the wall of al Khubdha, northwards from this, stands a very badly weathered monument (Fig. 117), generally called the " Corinthian " tomb from the fact that the capitals of its columns are—or are supposed to have been—of the Corinthian order. Next to this, northwards, stands an immense façade (Fig. 113), unique in its design as regards Petra, which is a copy, in arrangement, of the front of a Roman palace, and which it will be convenient to refer to simply as " the Palace." The German explorers called it the *Stockwerk-Grab*, and the French the *Trois-*

Étages, for reasons obvious from the photograph. I cannot make out, however, that it has at all certainly been a burial-place. Still further north, at the end of a projecting promontory of al Khubdha, is an ornate façade (Fig. 118) of a monument carrying a Latin inscription which has enabled its date to be guessed at as about A.D. 140, and which—with the arrangements of the interior—indicate that it was certainly a burial-place.

Further north than this tomb of Sextius Florentinus there appear to be no more classical carvings upon the Khubdha wall. Brünnow notes a classical monument (No. 647) near al Nasara, similar to that in Fig. 106. Unfortunately I did not see it. The courtyard in front of it appears to be visible in the 1923 Air survey. Most of the remaining classical monuments are to be found southwards from the opening of the Outer Siq along the western wall of the Obelisk ridge and in the Farasa and Numair Wadis. In the southern region I have not found any monuments of this type.

In the west there are only a few classical monuments. One is to be seen behind al Habis, close to the beginning of the ascent to the place of sacrifice on the ridge. The extraordinary weathering of the sandstone of al Habis into what look like water-worn pot-holes is very noticeable here.

In the lower part of the Wadi al Dair there is a triclinium (Fig. 112) (generally called the " Lion tomb," although it was not actually a tomb), and on the Dair plateau at the head of the Wadi is the largest of all the classical monuments, the Dair temple itself (Fig. 114). In the northward continuation of the Dair Wadi, above the point where the route to the Dair itself has branched to the left, is the monument of Fig. 119 with three urns. We found that the chamber of this monument contained a grave (filled up, though it still contained a few bones), but it was also obviously a triclinium, presumably for funeral feasts.

The monuments at Petra which are more or less purely Nabataean have interest as showing the ideas of a Semitic race, very much isolated geographically, but receiving and more or less assimilating from time to time suggestions from more highly civilised peoples received from Europe either directly or by way of Persia. The monuments of the classical type do not, I think, possess any such interest or importance. They show merely what the architect-constructors of Petra (by that time Roman subjects) could do, and did, with designs entirely foreign to them. They are little more than copies, more or less faithful, of western designs modified so that they could be carved out of the solid instead of being built up in masonry. Under these conditions it does not seem profitable to compare them, either metrically or critically, with Greco-Roman standards, as has been so frequently done in the published journals of visitors to the Wadi Musa, with an occasional affectation of vast critical superiority! Jaussen and Savignac* have compared in very great detail careful measurements of one of the great tomb-façades at Madaïn Salih with Greek standards, and have come to the conclusion that the rock-carvers must have been working closely to recognised Greek proportions. The great variation in the chief proportions of other monuments raises some doubt as to whether this conclusion would apply generally. I do not think, however, for the reasons which I have mentioned, that in any case the point is an important one. In what follows I will do no more than indicate, quite shortly, the general features of the principal Petraean examples of classical design applied to rock carvings.

The single classical monument in the Bab al Siq (No. 34 Br.) is that one which is oddly placed immediately below the Obelisk monument in Fig. 86. Its proportions are so squat as to indicate pretty clearly that it was constructed after the Obelisk monument above it had been already finished. The reason for choosing so awkward a position when there was the whole side of the valley to choose from must, I fear, remain unknown to us. One may suppose that the placing of its base on a platform

* *Mission Archéologique*, Vol. II., Chapter 3.

so high above the Wadi bottom as the photograph shows it to be must have been due to well-grounded fear of spate water in the Wadi Musa. During Miss Martineau's visit in the month of March, 1847, a sudden spate came down which for a while rendered crossing the stream (opposite the " Bint ") impossible. It was the water of this spate coming down the Siq which brought down the shrine with the Greek inscription in the Siq close to the Khazna, so that it is now somewhere below tons of fallen rock.*

Returning to the monument of Fig. 86, the six engaged columns supporting an ornate pediment with a decorated arched cornice (see also Fig. 122) are not more than about 12 feet high. A kind of attic, with the duplicated capitals as a second order, carries another pediment of ordinary type very much flattened down. The central chamber, about 21 feet broad by 24 feet deep, is a triclinium. The benches of the triclinium, which are about 7 feet broad, are rebated round their front edges by a ledge about a foot broad and 5 inches below their level, a feature which occurs in many of the Petraean triclinia, but not generally in such dimensions. Right and left of the door little flights of steps are placed to save the guests the trouble of scrambling up to the 3 feet height of the benches (as also in the case of Fig. 119). Somewhat high up in the back-wall are two deep recesses excavated as if to contain bodies, but only just over 5 feet deep. Dr. Dalman suggests that they might be intended as ossuaries of some sort. Two side chambers open from the cleared platform in front of the monument, but are not otherwise directly connected with the central monument itself. The left-hand chamber contains five graves. The chamber on the right is plain except for a shallow niche on its back-wall, but opens into a second inner chamber containing four graves, each apparently arranged for holding two coffins one above the other. On the opposite side of the Wadi, a little above the path, there appear also to be rock-cut graves (see Brünnow, Fig. 239), and above these come the lines of niches referred to later on (see Fig. 189), so that this part of the valley must have been considered, for some reason, to be a specially desirable burying-place.

In the Siq itself, about 400 yards from its western end, on the east wall of a cross ravine, is al Khazna (Fig. 121, No. 62 Br.), already mentioned, the so-called " Treasure-House of Pharaoh,"

---

* Miss Martineau is the only visitor to Petra who seems to have been fortunate enough to see what the Wadi Musa looked like when the river was really running. I think it worth while to quote the whole of her story—the year was 1847 and the month as late as March. She says, in returning from an expedition in the Northern district:

" I knew that the tents lay south-west, on the other side of the water-course. So off we went, as straight as an arrow —across gullies, over hills, through ankle-deep water, for it was no time for picking and choosing our footing. One of my companions was lame that day; but on he must go, over stone-heaps and through pools. We found a way down into the water-course, walked many yards along it, knowing now where we were, and got out of it not far from our platform. Within three minutes, before I had half put off my wet clothes, I heard a shout: the torrent had come down. Down it came, almost breast-high, rushing and swirling among the thickets and great stones in the water-course, giving us a river in a moment, where we had never dreamed of hoping to see one! As soon as I could, I ran out to the verge of the platform; and I shall never forget the sight. It was worth any inconvenience and disappointment. We forgot the dripping tent, from which little rills ran upon our bedsteads: we forgot the lost hours of this last day, and our damp wardrobes, and all our discomforts. There was the muddy torrent—or rather, the junction of two torrents, which divided the channel between them for some way—the one which had come from the Sîk, and past the theatre, being muddy, and the other, from the north-east, being clear. On came the double stream, bowing and waving the tamarisks and oleanders—the late quarters of the Arabs who were now looking on from the opposite bank. Just before sunset, I went to look again. The white waterfalls were still tumbling from the steeps; and the whole scene was lighted up by a yellow glow from the west, where the sky was clearing. The torrent was still dashing along, making eddies among the stones; and beyond it, in a thicket, under a wall of rock, was a group of Arabs round a fire, whose smoke curled up above the trees. At night, I went out once more; and that was the finest of all. The torrent was too deep within its banks to be touched by the moon, which was now shining brightly. The waters could scarcely be seen, except in one spot where they caught a gleam from an Arab fire. But at this hour, its rush seemed louder than ever." (The quotation is from Miss Martineau's *Eastern Life : Past and Present*, published in 1848.)

known also as al Jarra (the Urn) on account of the urn which surmounts it, and which has been traditionally supposed to contain the " treasure " and has in consequence been the target of many bullets in the vain hope that it could so be broken open. Of the six principal columns the two central (one of which has fallen) are entirely disengaged, the others are engaged in wing walls. Above the porch is a second storey divided into three parts, the wings surmounted by a broken pediment, which, however, returns into the wall of a deep central recess. In the centre is a circular tower, like a miniature temple, with a ring of columns supporting a coned roof over a heavy cornice. On the top of this stands the urn on a base which appears to be a replica of the capitals of the columns below. In the panels between the columns are statues now so much (intentionally) damaged that their original nature is almost unrecognisable. At various salient angles have also been animal figures, now equally unrecognisable. Domaszewski was able to take telephotographs of these (published in Brünnow, pp. 180-186), which show sufficient intelligible detail to enable him to make shrewd guesses at their original character and meaning. He considers that the principal figure—in the centre panel of the little round temple immediately above the pediment—is certainly intended for Isis. Below the principal cornices the flat surfaces are covered with decoration in low-relief, still well preserved. The capitals are of the Corinthian, and not the Nabataean, type.

With the help of a long ladder and a plucky Arab to climb it, Dr. Dalman was able to obtain, for the first time, the actual dimensions of this monument. I can, of course, only quote his figures; they are given fully in an essay in his second volume,* with a full and interesting description of the architectural details, and discussion as to their meaning. The columns are about 5 feet in diameter, so that the broken shaft in Fig. 120 is some 12 feet in height. The breadth of the façade is 92 feet, and the total height to the top of the urn 130 feet. The urn itself is about 11 feet high.

There are plain chambers right and left of the open hall, of which one contains a recess with hollows which look like graves. The great central chamber is nearly 40 feet square and about the same height. A small chamber, possibly unfinished, opens from it on each side, and in the back-wall, approached by three steps, is a plain chamber about 10 feet square. There are no definite graves anywhere visible, but it would be necessary to clear the floor of a considerable thickness of débris before it could be said certainly that none existed. Dr. Dalman notes that there is a curious basin-shaped hollow about a foot in diameter, having a discharge opening and rebated round its edge for a cover, in the centre of the threshold stone of the central chamber. Whether the monument was intended as a memorial temple or as a grave this basin would no doubt receive libations in honour of the king or the god from entrants or worshippers.

We have neither inscription nor tradition to indicate the probable age of the Khazna. From his identification of the central statue as Isis, and from the use of certain Egyptian features which he thinks are shown by his photographs, Domaszewski concludes that the building of the Khazna may have been due to Hadrian (*circa* A.D. 131), who, he states, included Egyptian gods in his pantheon. Dr. Dalman, on the other hand, differs (perhaps as a matter of course) from this conclusion, and in a long paper (published also in translation in the *Annual* of the Palestine Exploration Fund in 1911), argues that the Khazna is a " Temple tomb " of one of the later Nabataean kings who affected Greek ideas. The matter is too much one of pure opinion to be worth arguing about. But on general grounds, perhaps, the date of Hadrian would appear more likely to be too early than too late.

The use of Corinthian capitals, the elaborate mouldings, the decorative reliefs on the flat surfaces, the free use of statues and carved animals, are features so foreign to Nabataean conventions and workmanship that it can hardly have been either designed or carried out by the native Arabs. Its

* *Neue Petra Forschungen*, 1912, pp. 1-76, see specially Fig. 66.

cost, also, must necessarily have been very great, and all these considerations point to a time considerably later than the beginning of the Roman occupation.

There are evident points of similarity, as also of difference, between the Khazna and the " Corinthian tomb " and al Dair. I do not think, however, that valid arguments can be drawn from either resemblances or differences as to their relative dates of construction. All are based on foreign models, and may be supposed to have been carried out to the order of foreigners, with foreign designers, and possibly foreign workmen, and with no special reference to what happened to have been done before in Petra itself.

The " Urn tomb " (Fig. 116, No. 772 Br.) stands high up on the right bank of the outer Siq, in a deep recess carved into the wall of al Khubdha. The front of the recess is levelled out into a platform over 70 feet wide, on each side of which is a narrow cloister behind a row of plain-topped columns, like the similar arrangement in al Khan. The monument itself carries four tall pilasters on its face, two being half-round engaged columns, and the two outer ones (as in many other cases at Petra) composed of a flat-faced pilaster combined with a quarter column. The door has a classical architrave over two pilasters with Nabataean capitals, with triglyphs separated by pateræ. The pilasters have, so far as can be distinguished, capitals of the Nabataean type. The attic is so weathered away that its details are hardly distinguishable; the general appearance is that of reduplicated capitals, as in many cases of Nabataean monuments. The whole is, as with al Khazna and al Dair, surmounted by an urn. The interior is a huge chamber about 62 feet wide and 56 feet deep, with a number of recesses at the back, one on the left wall and two on the right. The back recesses have been reduced to three by removing subdivisions, and the hall has been used at some time for Christian worship. On one panel of the back-wall it carries a painted inscription in Greek referring to a Bishop whose time is identified as 447 A.D., and this, if correct, appears to be the latest date which we can connect certainly with life in Petra. From the photograph it will be seen that there is a second chamber above the principal one. I fear that this, like many other upper chambers, has remained unexamined. Fig. 116 shows how the court in front had been supported on arches in two tiers, one above the other.

Within a short distance of this monument on the slopes below it, Mr. Philby and I found and unearthed in 1923 the fine Roman jar of Fig. 120. This vase is about 24 inches in diameter and 20 inches high, with a thickness of 2 to $2\frac{1}{4}$ inches. It has a hole of 2 to 3 inches diameter in the bottom, and has two stout ears.

Further round the wall of al Khubdha stands the " Corinthian tomb " of Fig. 117 (No. 766 Br.), which has many points in common with the Khazna. It is over 80 feet in breadth. It has been terribly destroyed by rock falls and weathering. The front has eight round pilasters or engaged columns, having what are held to be (but I do not feel very certain as to this) Corinthian capitals. Above the cornice over the columns is an attic filled apparently with duplicate capitals, and over this two wing blocks, and a central circular tower as in the Khazna. The centre doorway, entirely broken out, opens into the left-hand side of a chamber, roughly 30 feet by 40 feet, having three large niches in the back-wall and several in the right-hand wall. Each of the three doors in the left-hand half of the façade opens into a quite plain separate chamber.

Next to the last-named monument, against the wall of al Khubdha, here facing north-west, stands the " Palace " of Fig. 113* (No. 765 Br.), the upper storey or storeys of which (having been constructed in masonry owing to the absence of rock) have to a great extent fallen away altogether. The scheme of this façade differs altogether from all the rest, and appears to be an attempt to copy

* This figure shows also the Corinthian tomb on its right-hand side.

the appearance of a Roman palace. It has four doorways, each enclosed by a pair of high pilasters, the cornices on which support a plain frieze. Above this is a complete second order of eighteen pilasters, and above these again an attic (now remaining only at the right-hand end), surmounted by other storeys no longer in existence. The four doors open into four separate rectangular chambers, of which the two central ones have a short communicating passage. The second of the chambers, about 33 feet by 23 feet, has a large shallow recess about 12 feet wide and 3 feet deep covering a great part of one side-wall, and another similar one in the back-wall. The four grave-like recesses in the back-wall sketched in Brünnow's Fig. 431 do not seem to exist.* It is always possible, in view of the amount of rubbish that covers the floor of many of the Petraean chambers, that there are actually graves in the floors. But apart from this there are no signs at all of the " Palace " having been used for burials. It is noteworthy that the Egyptian Sultan Bibars, in the fifteenth century, seems to have accepted the Petraean chambers as suitable for dwelling-places (see p. 36, *ante*).

In the cliff immediately to the left of the " Palace " a large tank has been excavated, with steps leading down to the bottom of it. An unfortunate accident destroyed my photograph of this, but I think its depth was about 8 feet. It may have been only a reservoir, but perhaps also a bath. In front of its outer wall, and facing the valley, were several deep recesses, each large enough to push a body into if they were used as graves. I did not, however, find any traces here of a place used for religious purposes, such as in most cases is found near any large group of graves.

The wall of al Khubdha is destitute of monuments for the next 300 yards, when another important classical monument (Fig. 118, No. 763 Br.) occurs, the last classical monument in this direction. A Latin inscription here has been deciphered as naming a Roman officer, Sextius Florentinus, supposed by Laborde to have lived about the time of Antoninus Pius. The photograph shows the ornate nature of the façade as well as its ruined condition allows. The chamber contains five grave niches in its back-wall and two in the right-hand wall, besides a small chamber, possibly a shrine.

The tomb of Florentinus has been made at the end of a somewhat narrow promontory projecting from the west face of al Khubdha. The aeroplane map of 1923 showed that there was a flat area like a large courtyard on the ridge of this promontory, and we found that this court was approachable by cut steps on both sides (see next Chapter). The court proved to be a starting-place for a very carefully engineered ascent to the sacrificial places on the top of al Khubdha. One can well imagine that the court was the place of assembly for the celebrants, who would, on any great occasion, climb the long steps to the top in single file.

Of the same general type as the Khazna, the Urn Temple, and the Corinthian Tomb, is the immense monument known as al Dair—the " Convent " (Fig. 114). This temple stands on a rocky plateau about 560 feet above the level of the Qasr al Bint, reached by a scramble up narrow and most picturesque gullies, which may be called collectively the Wadi al Dair, and in which the ascent is much facilitated by flights of steps not yet entirely worn away. The total width of the façade of the Dair is 154 feet, and its height about 132 feet. (The width of the west front of Westminster Abbey is about 100 feet.) Its central section contains six engaged columns, three on each side of the doorway, with a second order above carrying two wings, and a broken and returned pediment with a central circular tower surmounted by a gigantic urn (Fig. 125) having a total height of over 30 feet. It will be seen from the photograph that this urn is supported by a gigantic duplication

* Brünnow marks this plate " Verbessert nach Laborde pl. 59." I have, unfortunately, only obtained the English edition of Laborde, which has been most unworthily treated by a very futile—and, happily, nameless—translator and editor, and does not contain the plate in question.

of a Nabataean capital. In general arrangement the second storey is very much like the upper part of the Khazna, but with much less decoration. Beyond the central portion stand two wings faced by flat pilasters worked into quarter columns as in the case of Fig. 116. There are two shallow niches in the lower storey and three in the upper, but none of them show signs of ever having been filled with statuary or images of any kind. The immense doorway, 26 feet high, opens into a single great chamber about 38 feet square and 33 feet high, quite without decoration, and carrying only on its back-wall a high shallow niche the bottom of which is reached by a short run of four steps on each side. The back-wall of the niche has marks which indicate that an idol block or a small altar once stood in it. Whichever it was, it has entirely disappeared, but its previous existence indicates that the building was a temple and not a tomb. On the wall of the niche several small crosses have been carved, and we know from inscriptions found lower down in the Dair Wadi (see p. 77) that this was a place of pilgrimage as late as Christian times. It seems strange that nothing more should have been left here to indicate a place of Christian worship than some roughly scored or painted crosses a few inches high. Of course, it may well be that any more notable Christian symbol, if there ever was one on the altar, would have been destroyed by Moslems just as readily as the idol block.

The great mass of rock out of which the Dair has been carved has been of such dimensions that the carved sides of the wings are carried up clear of the great recess, and from any distance appear actually as if they were side-walls of the main structure. I think this is a unique feature in the Petraean wall monuments.

Dr. Dalman points out, as curious, that the doorway is not truly opposite the central altar niche, but some 2 feet to one side, and deduces from this that the doorway was so placed in order to throw better direct sunlight on the altar at certain times. I fear this reasoning would involve the assumption that the doorway was opened out after the altar niche had been carved, which hardly seems possible.

We shall see reasons later on to think that this plateau of al Dair may well have been a holy place from very early Petraean times, and on through the Roman occupation, even until Christianity had become the national religion of Rome.

I found only three other classical monuments on the western rocks of Petra, although it is quite probable that a few more have escaped notice.

Near the foot of the Wadi al Dair, at the head of a short ravine branching to the left, stands the monument of Fig. 112 (No. 452 Br.), which has been called the "Lion tomb," but which is in fact a triclinium, and not a grave. It owes its name to the fact that two small lions in low-relief, not very visible in the photograph, are carved one on each side of the door. More notable is the fact that beside it, on the left, there is a shallow niche containing the block symbol of Dusares, although the elaborate frieze and the engraved decoration between the wings of the capitals would indicate a somewhat late date in Roman times for its construction. The appearance of the doorway indicates the probable original existence of a circular opening or window above it.

Considerably higher up the ravine, beyond the point where the Wadi al Dair turns westward, there stands on the right-hand (east) side a severely classical façade (Fig. 119). The photograph shows more clearly than in most cases the shape of the Nabataean capitals and the compound section of the side pilasters. The three urns are still standing on the pediment. The chamber has benches on the two sides obviously for feasting purposes, each bench being reached by a little flight of four steps against the front wall. At the left-hand corner three steps lead from the bench up to a small chamber in the back. On removing some of the débris from the floor we found a grave in the right-

I

hand half of the floor extending under the back-wall. The grave was rebated round the edge for a stone cover. In it there were still two small bones.* This monument is not shown in Brünnow's map. Fig. 119 is a good example of the way in which lines of interstratified white sandstone weather very much faster than the harder red-coloured rock.

The photograph No. 119 shows perhaps more clearly than any other the design of what I have called the Nabataean capital. This design (a sort of crude Ionic) is singularly persistent through every type of monument at Petra, extending also even to the whole of the classical monuments, with the exception of the Khazna and two or three others. Even the severely classical Dair temple and the Lion triclinium have these capitals with only very slight modifications.

The remainder of the classical monuments are to be found chiefly on the western wall of the Obelisk ridge and in the region of the Farasa and Numair Wadis. Fig. 122 (No. 229 Br.), on the Obelisk ridge, is one of the most ornate and one of the best preserved of these. Its special feature is the moulded arch (with urns) as a mere decoration on the front, carried over the architrave of the door on two tall pilasters.

The striking monument (Fig. 124, No. 228 Br.) is carved on a rock projecting at right-angles from the Obelisk ridge, and therefore faces north. It is approached by the steps shown in the photograph from a platform which is itself reached by broad steps from the general level. On this platform are two tanks, one square and one octagonal, and these, with the special approaches, would seem to indicate that the monument, although primarily a tomb, may have been also a place of some special regard or sanctity. The right-hand wall of this tomb is of particular interest in that it has been marked out with a series of panels between pilasters in low-relief, each panel being apparently intended in due course to be excavated to serve as a burial chamber. Such excavation has, in fact, taken place in the case of the four panel-sections nearest the back-wall, and it may be suggested that this mausoleum has actually served to receive the remains of only four members of a family which expected to occupy at least a dozen cavities. Some very serious cause would appear to be necessary to explain the abandonment of a chamber with such external pretensions (the façade, the stairway, and the two tanks on the platform in front of it) to importnce. The partition between the last two loculi has been broken down so completely that the two virtually form a single chamber, and an apparent grooving of the sides of the pilasters on either side of the loculi may have served to hold a wooden or metal shutter designed to shut off the occupied cavities from the chamber. The back-wall is entirely plain, but the left-hand wall is adorned with an arched recess of considerable dimensions, though it contains no indication of the use to which it may have been put.

The photograph shows that there is a second chamber, of considerable size, beside, although in communication with, the main chamber. Both chambers show the lintel notches for the door and one, if not both, had window openings above the door.

The first, or northern, of the two Farasa Wadis opens a little south of the last described monument; the mouth of the valley is crossed by a masonry wall, obviously the remains of a water-retaining barrage. In the open part of the valley above this are two monuments of classical design which have special interest.

Fig. 128 is a view of the interior of a hall with fluted pilasters on the north side of the Wadi (No. 235 Br.). It is the only one of the Petraean rock chambers which has internal architectural decoration of this type. (There are, however, several chambers of which the walls still retain traces of fresco painting. The most notable of these is in al Barid, and is described in Chapter I.) This monument, whatever its purpose may have been, has no architectural façade. We may,

* As to a triclinium being also a grave, see pp. 34 and 52, *ante.*

therefore, assume that it was never intended to have any, for many examples indicate that the external work on these monuments preceded even the opening up of the doorway.

The chamber is about 35 feet square. The back-wall and each of the side-walls is divided into five bays by fluted pilasters or engaged columns. (The fluting was unfortunately not very visible in the light by which the photograph was taken.) In each bay of the side-walls is a niche placed like a window (as seen in Fig. 128) some feet from the ground. The niches in the back-wall extend like doors right down to the ground (as seen in Fig. 302 Br.). One of them, in the centre, is double, and one has been opened through at some time as if for a grave. All except this one are merely a few inches deep. Above some of the niches are straight grooves apparently once filled with stone of a quality different from that of the walls. The front-wall is quite plain on the inside, but has three door openings and also windows, of which one is seen in the photograph. It is not possible to do any more than guess at the intention or function of this remarkable monument. It may be compared with the hall on the east side of al Habis (Fig. 134) which has a door with two windows on each side of it, and which (like the Farasa monument) has no external decoration, although it has had a good deal of squaring done at the doorway and window openings. The chamber on al Habis is smaller (about 33 feet by 21 feet), but had certainly a second storey chamber, lit by a window, above it (see p. 63).

Opposite the pillar hall stands the monument of Fig. 129 (No. 233 Br.), which has become known as the Statue tomb. It is of quite straightforward classical design, with four pilasters and a plain frieze and pediment. In the three bays into which the columns divide the front are niches with statues, but the nature of the figures represented is not very certain. Beyond the façade window openings have been roughly cut out on both sides. The monument contains two chambers, in one of which are four arch-topped niches, probably for burials.

Above this monument, but quite unconnected with it, is a rock terrace on the wall of which are a number of niches at two levels, which must have been connected with some religious worship. The four lower niches (seen in the photograph) are similar to those along a ledge on the eastern face of al Habis, seen in Fig. 133 (p. 62).

The inner part of the northern Farasa Wadi is reached by a stairway up the very narrow passage on the left of Fig. 123. Immediately to the north of the opening stands the Temple (No. 244 Br.), shown in the photograph, which is approached by steps, and which is fronted by a large cleared, level space—once, no doubt, green with plants and trees. This monument is one of the very few in Petra which have free columns with a portico. (Other examples are al Khan in the Bab al Siq (p. 72), and the Khazna in the Siq itself, as well as one (Fig. 56) in the district of al Barid.) The portico itself is about 24 feet by 20 feet, and opens into a plain chamber 18 feet square, having a window on the south side. There is no sign of any burial in the chamber, but in the portico there lies or stands a stone about 3 feet long by 1 foot broad, like a gravestone with a rounded top, on the face of which is lightly carved in an oval a figure which has been called a cross, but which, in fact, resembles a star with three (not four) triangular arms, the apices of the triangles meeting in the centre.* Above this monument or temple, and approached from the Wadi by steps still existing, are unmistakable signs of worship, which will be described further on, and with which the Temple may well have been connected.

The Roman city which flourished for several centuries, and once covered both banks of the Wadi Musa, is now represented practically only by ruins. The sites of at least two temples are

---

* Dalman gives a photograph of this stone on p. 196. Brünnow's sketch (probably from memory), shows four arms as a cross.

indicated by their fallen columns, and also the probable site of baths. Portions of masonry walls indicate that the main water-course was once " regulated," and in places arched over. But looked at merely as a *Roman* city, Petra does not possess any interest comparable with that of Jarash, or even of Amman.

The one building left standing, or partly standing, is that known as the Qasr al Bint (Fig. 126), or Qasr Bint Fir'un (the palace of the daughter of Pharaoh), (No. 403 Br.). It stands near the entrance to the Siyagh, and under the rock of al Habis, the so-called " Acropolis." From its decoration, by means of plaster plaques pinned on to the masonry, it may be supposed to be a fairly late Roman work, and in any case can hardly have been erected before A.D. 106, when the Romans took possession of Petra. The pronaos is quite open, with four columns of 6 feet 6 inches diameter. In its back-wall, which is virtually the front-wall of the Temple, is the huge arch of 20-feet span shown separately in Fig. 127. Behind this the building seems to have been open across its whole breadth (about 95 feet) for a distance of some 33 feet, and further back to have been divided into three bays of which the two side ones had apparently a second storey, reached by stairways in the wall. The back part of the building had massive double walls only about 3 feet apart, a construction the object of which is not now intelligible. It has been frequently suggested that the existence of the upper storeys favours the idea that the building was rather a dwelling-place than a temple, but the reasoning seems inconclusive. A peculiar arrangement of masonry (which originally must have been quite covered by the external shell) is seen in the base of the western wall. I have not seen it noticed before, and am unable to suggest any reason for it.

At a slightly lower level than the Temple, and between it and the river bed, stands the large masonry altar, which is shown in Fig. 134. This is a mass of masonry some 40 feet square, with a square hollow in its centre.

Brünnow gives a schematic restoration of the whole Temple, with dimensioned plan and sections, which should be referred to for details.

From the altar the line of a made road can be traced eastwards through the remains of the triple archway of Fig. 130 (No. 406 Br.). The piers of the archway were once decorated with applied plaques like the Temple, and the stones now lying all round them show moulded carvings. From the archway the line of road was bordered on the north by columns, of which the bases only are left, as far at least as a great square clearing which may have been the forum. This clearing seems to have been a natural level, completed on the eastern side by a natural wall or cliff, and on the south partly, I think, by masonry. On the north would come the colonnade just referred to, while on the west the level runs out into the open valley.

As regards physical magnitude the greatest relic of Roman work is naturally the theatre (Fig. 131, No. 161 Br.). No doubt the constructors had good reason for the enormous excavation which they made in order to get the required slope of the seats. But it is not obvious why the much steeper natural slope should not have been retained. There are thirty-three rows of seats, and the diameter of the inner row at the stage-level has been measured as 125 feet. If the dimensions are correct the seating capacity has not been exaggerated as between 3,000 and 4,000. The great openings seen in the back-wall are obviously chambers of tombs or other monuments which have been cut through to gain the required dimensions. The proscenium has disappeared, a few fragments of columns only remain on the ground, and what is apparently an entrance to a blind corridor.

All photographs of the theatre taken from near the ground-level give it, inevitably, the flat appearance of Fig. 131. Seen from a height, as from al Khubdha, its proportions are much better seen, and it is shown to cover more nearly a half-circle (Fig. 182).

One other relic of the post-Nabataean period, only, remains to be separately mentioned—the so-called columbarium of Fig. 132. This peculiar piece of work is on the eastern wall of al Habis, behind and above the Qasr al Bint. The " pigeon-holes " are each about 10 inches square and nearly the same depth, the top surface being curved downwards at the back. They cover the front as well as the walls of the interior chamber. Many of them are now choked up altogether, and a number which appear quite open in Brünnow's Fig. 330 (taken about thirty years ago) are seen to be filled up in Mr. Philby's photograph taken in the spring of 1924. Dr. Dalman, arguing from other examples which he has seen in the East, and which are undoubtedly pigeon-houses, considers that this also must be for pigeons, or doves. Dr. Post, in the Quarterly Statement of the Palestine Exploration Fund for 1888, describes and illustrates a columbarium found somewhere west of Amman, near Araq al Amir, which very closely resembles the Petra monument. Mr. Forder, who has paid many visits to Petra, is quoted as saying in a Chicago magazine that there are beautiful columbaria, " some with finely-chased portals, hidden away in the side valleys," but I have not been fortunate enough to come across any of them.

The earlier visitors to Petra all noticed a high arch spanning the Siq, not many yards from its eastern entrance. This arch, according to Mr. Gray Hill, fell down in 1896. It was of a single span only, resting on the sides of the gorge, but decorated abutments were carved, purely as orna- ments, upon the walls, and the traces of these can still be seen, although they require to be looked for. Notes of early travellers about this construction are rather amusing: it is absolutely inaccessible from below; an easy flight of steps in the rock lead up to it; it contains obvious provision for carrying water; there is no possibility of getting any water to or from it ! I think it is pretty certain that it was merely decorative, although perhaps hardly " triumphal," and not intended for any use either for passengers or for water.

V.—MONUMENTS CONNECTED WITH CULT

On matters connected with the cultural remains at Petra Dr. Dalman's book* is, and must always remain, invaluable, even if it is not so absolutely exhaustive of the subject as he assumed it to be. On his several visits to Petra—during which his itineraries show a much-to-be-envied activity —he tells us that he has himself seen as many as a hundred and eighty block idols. He has also identified, described, and given sketch-plans of a very large number of what he considers to be places of worship, and calls " holy places " (*Heiligtümer*). He applies this name only to places where he finds a whole group of cultural objects together, among which he includes sacred stones, niches with idols, shrines and altars, basins, and arrangements for feasts. He adds very truly that no particular arrangement of such objects can be predicated as being the only proper, or even the general, one, but that no two " holy places " are alike in their details.

Dealing even with a subject-matter so closely limited, his treatise greatly exceeds in length the whole of this book, in which I have to cover a very much wider ground. For those, and I hope there may be some in future, who wish to study Petraean monuments with a special view to their cultural uses and signification, Dr. Dalman's book will be an absolute necessity. My object here is only to give some idea of the various objects in Petra which appear to be connected in any way with worship, without special regard as to whether they are combined into a " holy place " of any sort or not. Such objects appear to be distributed almost as widely over the whole area of the Petraean remains as Methodist chapels in the Midlands. (Strabo says the Nabataeans were very

* *Petra und seine Felsheiligtümer*, Leipzig, 1908.

religious.) They are to be found north and south of the Bab al Siq, in al Ramla and al Madras, in the outer Siq, on the summit and western face of al Khubdha, and about al Nasara—southward on the Obelisk ridge and in the Farasa district and on to the watershed, westward on al Habis and in the Siyagh, on the plateau of al Dair, and on the ridges and valleys of al Ma'aisara, as well as far north in al Baidha and al Barid. Everything within the actual city walls, beyond the remains of columns indicating the probable site of temples, is, of course, too entirely destroyed to be recognisable. The still standing Roman " temple in antis " near al Habis I have described as a classical monument (Fig. 126), but I do not include Roman remains as affecting Nabataean cult. It is interesting to notice, however, that in such situations as the Farasa Wadi, Jabal Numair, the Dair Wadi and plateau, and others, there are indications that the Nabataean worship, whatever it may have been, was continued after the city became Roman:—to every country its own gods.

The neighbourhood of al Habis and the Siyagh must have been a place of considerable sanctity many centuries before the Roman Temple came into existence. On the top of the northern and lower end of the ridge of al Habis there is a small cleared area (approached by steps by a little ravine on the west which starts beside a classical tomb) which forms a plateau in front of a great carefully squared block, no doubt regarded as a natural altar. Special stepways allow the top of the block to be reached for sacrifices. Beside the clearing are various indications of its use for worship of some sort, a small rounded sacellum, a niche-basin and a small tank, which together bring it within Dalman's definition of a " holy place." Its roughness and simplicity in comparison with some others indicate that it may be, like similar places on al Ma'aisara west of the Wadi Turkamaniya, among the oldest Petraean places of worship which are still at all recognisable. It is practically only accessible by the one route mentioned above, being inaccessible from the higher, or southern, end of al Habis.

It is easy to make a circuit of al Habis either round its north or its south end. The former route is the more interesting from our present point of view. Its commencement is shown in Figs. 133 and 134. Almost immediately beyond the Roman Temple there is visible somewhat high up on the east wall of al Habis a large cave with squared entrance, but without any façade. In front of it is a peculiarly-shaped isolated block which may possibly have been invested with some special significance. The cave is approached—or was once approachable—by a ledge to the south of it, the wall of which carries a row of five shallow niches like those (also along a ledge) above the Roman tomb in the Farasa Wadi, Fig. 129 (p. 59). It is singular that this line of niches is more often invisible than visible from below, according, of course, to the incidence of the light. I had looked at the wall many times before I saw them, and I have several photographs in which they are perfectly invisible. I believe it would be analogous to modern Moslem custom that a prayer should be said in passing the niches, or in passing each niche—that they should be treated, in fact, like the " Stations of the Cross " in the route to a Calvary.

Fig. 134 represents the wall of al Habis immediately to the right of Fig. 133. In the foreground is the great masonry Roman altar which stands close to the river bed in front of the Temple (p. 60). Behind it, beyond the left of the photograph, is the large cave with the row of niches mentioned above (Fig. 133). Almost immediately below this cave there starts a long ramp running up the face of the wall northwards, a ledge partly natural and partly artificial. It passes, below a great white patch, the half-choked open grave in the back of which is the corbelled niche of Fig. 67 with the carved symbols above it. A little higher up, just before the ledge rounds the northern corner of the rock, it passes below the remarkable chamber or hall, seen in Fig. 134 (No. 400 Br.), with a doorway and four windows making it like the front of a house, which is always conspicuous in views of this end of al Habis or of the opening of the Siyagh. The chamber itself is rectangular, about 36 by 20 feet, and its walls carry most beautiful natural markings in coloured bands. About 6 feet of the length at its south end is marked off by projecting wings, of which one is seen in the photograph of the interior (Fig. 135). The two southern windows, but only one of the northern windows, open into the hall. The northern end of the hall opens by a doorway into a small chamber about 7 feet by 10 feet, unlighted. Above this small chamber is a floor which at one time has been a kind of gallery at the end of the hall, quite open to the south. At some time this gallery has been converted into a separate chamber by building the existing masonry wall across the front of it, in which a doorway (now only accessible by a ladder) has been carefully constructed. The floor of this upper chamber is practically on a level with the bottom of the windows, so that it is lighted by the northern window. The appearance of the hall indicates that at one time the upper floor may have been continuous, making the whole a two-storey building. There are signs of plaster or stucco, which may probably at one time have covered the whole walls, in various places. The hall has never possessed any façade, but the jambs and lintel of the doorway have been carefully squared, although they are now much destroyed. The window openings also, although much damaged, appear to have been squared, and it is likely that the whole front was originally dressed, although without architectural ornament or features. Considering the very large number of perfectly plain chambers which have probably been used for habitations it can hardly be supposed that this elaborate " house " can have been intended merely for living in. More probably it may have been a meeting or assembly room connected with functions or celebrations in one of the special sites to be found further on.

The ramp turns the corner of the Siyagh ravine carefully protected by a low wall of rock left on its outer edge. A few yards further on, on the left-hand (or inner side) of the path, there is a circular hollow about 12 feet in diameter recessed into the cliff, its front still closed to a considerable extent by a natural block. It has obviously been a cistern, and a number of rectangular holes round its circumference, about 4 feet 6 inches from the ground, were no doubt connected with the fixing of a wooden cover upon it.

On the same wall, not much further round, is another " house " with a window on each side of its doorway. This contains only a rough chamber about 28 feet long and varying from 6 to 8 feet in width. Fig. 136 shows that it is very rough in appearance, and has obviously never had the trouble taken with its construction that must have been given to the other.

Fig. 137, taken looking down the opening of the Siyagh from a little distance to the eastward, shows the north end of al Habis, the " House " of Figs. 134 and 135, and the guarded ledge running round the rock. The rough front of Fig. 136 is in the shadow, hardly visible.

Continuing the traverse of the ledge, where it turns round to the north-west face of al Habis, one looks down across a little bay in the side of the Siyagh to the promontory seen in the middle of Fig. 137, which presents several interesting features to be presently discussed. Still further on, on the little ridge seen above the promontory in Fig. 137, there are the remains of a large tank or cistern, some 40 or 50 feet long (I am sorry I did not note the measurements at the time) and about 6 feet broad, its outer wall (overlooking the entrance of the Thughra Wadi) being mostly destroyed.

From this point there becomes visible the remarkable " garden-court " of Fig. 138. (The middle of the photograph, on the left-hand side, shows the continuation of the route round al Habis.) This court is reached from the higher level by the broad steps which are visible beyond it, and from the ravine below by other flights of steps now largely destroyed. In the north-west corner (the right-hand in the photograph) is the corniced tomb (containing a manger grave) of Fig. 80. The other openings in the west and south walls lead only to small plain chambers. The choked-up monument of Fig. 74, with the rectilinear decoration, stands in the south-east corner of the court, diagonally opposite to the visible corniced tomb. Its base, however, is some 6 feet above the floor of the court, and the lower flight of steps leading down to the court (out of sight in the photograph) practically cuts it off. There can be little doubt that it was carved out long before the court was excavated, and belongs to an earlier period. On the grassy platform immediately north of the court stands a huge isolated block, which has been for some reason squared out, and on which there has been cut out a small niche containing a block image.

On the west of the court, beyond the right-hand side of Fig. 138, and at the level of the top of the rock-wall, stands one of the most interesting and complete of the sacella of Petra, the triclinium of Fig. 139, discovered by Libbey and Hoskins in 1902. The rocks which appear so close behind the triclinium in the photograph are in reality a quarter of a mile away, on the eastern face of Biyara. The triclinium is an irregular rectangle about 16 feet by 12 feet, its sides having the rebated edges mentioned before. In the centre of the end is a raised portion which may have carried an altar or a symbolic block, or which may merely have been a place on which worshippers could put their offerings. Dr. Dalman finds, in connection with this triclinium, at slightly different levels, several of the adjuncts which he considers essential to a " holy place," and therefore admits the whole into that category. Southwards from the triclinium, and only visible from its further side, there is a chamber (Fig. 140) with a large window beside its door, once approachable by a broad flight of steps now mostly destroyed, and other chambers which I was unable to investigate. Somewhat to the south of these monuments again, the route round al Habis passes the great natural block of Fig. 141, which contains a plain chamber only, but has four niches on its front wall. It has also, on the south end, a cleared shelf with a flight of steps leading to it, but not now containing whatever object may have been originally there, and approachable by the steps.

With this block there ends, so far as my observation has gone, the series of cultural objects on al Habis. The walk round the southern end of the rock passes nothing of special interest (although there is not a single yard at Petra which has not its own interest), until the Columbarium (Fig. 132) is reached, just short of the south side of the Roman Temple, on the eastern face.

The Siyagh itself contains signs of cult in several places. On the right bank are several series of niches, blocks, basins, etc., which Dr. Dalman considers worthy of inclusion among holy places. One of these is represented in Fig. 142. Adjoining this, on the same terrace above the bottom of the water-course, is the long line of plain rock chambers of Fig. 63, which may well represent the lodging-places of those who had to attend the local ceremonials.

On the right bank of the Siyagh, close to its opening, are several large caves, in the walls of which numerous loculi or niches have been made. Fig. 64 is one of the largest of these; it has three plain recesses on the right side, three on the back, and four on the left side. None of these niches resembles either a shrine or a grave. Similar arrangements (see Figs. 83 and 84) in the outer Siq and in al Baidha may probably belong to traders coming into or leaving Petra, and using the place as a khan or serai. It is not likely, however, that the Siyagh was ever directly a route to or from Petra, so that this interpretation does not seem so probable here; but the use of the cave either for cultural purposes or for burials seems also unlikely. The cave never possessed a façade of any kind.

A little further on in the Siyagh the promontory mentioned above comes into view. Seen from a higher level east of the Siyagh this is shown in Fig. 137 and seen from the foot in Fig. 143. Looked down upon from the route round al Habis (Fig. 144), the top of the rock has all the appearance of a natural altar—probably also artificially stepped. The naturally contoured rock terraces round it (Fig. 145) look as if they had been artificially improved, so that they might form convenient sitting-places for seeing any ceremonials below. The front (east side) of the rock (Fig. 143) contains a large open cave with several niches on its back-wall and a large deep niche outside on the right. This cave was approached from the left by a ledge now destroyed, with the help of steep step-ways cut in the angle seen in Fig. 145, in which a few of the steps are still visible. On the spot these steps are quite visible, and go far up the rock, probably quite to the top, but they do not show themselves clearly in the shadow in the photographs. On the floor of the Siyagh, close to the foot of this rock, I found the remarkable isolated stone grave of Fig. 146 nearly hidden behind bushes. Looking back on the rock, from a point lower down the Siyagh, a flight of steps will be seen on the southern wall, and I found that these steps led to an open cave in the wall of which was a corbelled niche like that in Fig. 67. This cave must be more or less at the back of the cave of Fig. 143. Whether or not the top of the rock was utilised as an altar it seems obviously highly probable that the whole spot was of some special sanctity, if only on account of the two remarkable graves close by it, or their occupants.

As a matter of interest, but not as one connected in any way with the cult just suggested, I may note that a few yards further on in the Siyagh I found on its floor a frustrum of a stone column about 30 inches in diameter. Signs of quarrying further down the gully indicate that building material for the city may have been obtained here, and possibly during the dry weather the floor of the Siyagh has been used as a mason's yard.

The remaining cultural sites on the western side of Petra are chiefly in the Dair Wadi and on the Dair plateau. The triclinium of the lions (Fig. 112) has been already mentioned. It is specially of interest because it gives us a niche containing a Nabataean block symbol standing beside a late Roman monument; this will be seen just on the left of the façade. Higher up the Dair Wadi, near the foot of a very long flight of steps, a ravine falls in from the north, which is known as Qattar al Dair, and of which the opening is shown in Fig. 28. The most notable feature of this little wadi is a series of four tanks or cisterns, the largest about 10 feet by 7 feet, and an open triclinium of considerable dimensions. It contains also a number of the smaller common cultural objects, as well as an engraved two-armed cross and an illegible inscription. Some of the early visitors to Petra, finding this ravine full of greenery have expressed an enthusiasm for its rich beauty which must be accounted for by the bareness of the landscape everywhere else.

The long flight of steps above the Qattar ends in a small, comparatively level, plateau. On an eminence on the right of this, not very easy to identify, steps lead to a cave which has been called the Hermitage (*Klause*), on account of the Christian symbols and writing on its wall. On the left a ravine opens downwards to the Siyagh, and has correspondingly been given the name of Hermitage Gully. At its head are two very complicated " holy places " discovered by Musil, and minutely described, with sketch-plans, by Dalman. Another flight of steps and a short scramble upwards over some slabs take one to the plateau in front of al Dair (Fig. 114) already described (see pp. 56 and 57). Scattered over the plateau are a number of not very important places of cult found first by Musil and afterwards carefully investigated and more correctly located by Dalman. The wall on which many of these are placed (Fig. 147) extends to the left (west) of al Dair. The most interesting of them is a very rough relief of two camels and men, of which I was unfortunately not able to secure a photograph.

In the centre of the plateau is a rocky hummock on the surface of which are the ruins (fallen columns, etc.) of a Roman Temple. Nothing is left in place except a shrine niche of classical design at the back of a very large open chamber about 50 feet by 28 feet, with walls carefully worked square,

K

which must have formed a part of a large building of which the lines of fallen columns lie in front of it. These ruins have a counterpart near Madaïn Salih, where Jaussen was able to trace the whole arrangement of a temple from its fallen remains.

In the front of the left (north) wall of the clearing before al Dair there is a somewhat primitive altar (not visible in the photograph) approached by steps. Beside the flight of steps which leads up this wall to the level of the Urn there are also other cultural objects which indicate the probability that the Dair plateau was a "holy place" to which pilgrims came long before the great Temple was carved.

I have been greatly puzzled by a quotation from Miss Martineau's book (given by Brünnow) which makes her say that continuing an ascent above the Urn she came upon a place where there was a stone circle, or circle of stones. On examination we found the rocks above the Urn to be so difficult even for practised climbers that it was quite certain that Miss Martineau did not ascend them. Referring to her book I find that Brünnow had misunderstood what she had written. Dean Stanley also did the same when he quoted it, so the German professor is to be pardoned. The "circle of stones" referred to was looked down upon, not from the top of the Dair, but from the top of the central hummock opposite it, and represented the broken remains of the columns of the Roman temple mentioned above, which do not, however, in reality, form any *circle*. The narrow precipitous ridge further on mentioned by Miss Martineau I have not been able to identify. The high point from which Miss Martineau obtained the view she describes is seen on the right-hand of Brünnow's plate No. 366.

As compared with the region behind al Habis the huge area of the Ma'aisara Wadis and ridges is poor in places of cult. On the edge of the eastern bank of the Wadi Wastani there are the remains of a large open-air triclinium (Fig. 148), hardly recognisable through a covering of scrub. The rough block which is seen at its head may be there, I think, only accidentally. Within the area enclosed by the triclinium are at least half a dozen excavations which appear to be graves, but some of which may have been tanks or cisterns, and show signs of having been cemented. Our Arabs insisted that they were graves.

Just before reaching the row of four corniced monuments of Fig. 110, a narrow gully opens up on the right, and close beyond the head of this gully is the great court (Fig. 149) in front of the imposing monument of Fig. 106. The chamber in this monument contains seven large (vertical) niches or loculi—one of them being surmounted by an architrave—and one smaller niche, 2 feet from the ground, either for an idol or for gifts. On the right of the façade very large rock faces have been worked into smooth vertical walls, but no carving has been started on them. A second platform, about 4 feet higher than the level of the court, extends towards the edge of the Wadi al Tarfani, and gives access, beyond the point visible in Fig. 149, by a well-made flight of steps to the upper part of the ridge. At the head of these steps is the small stibadium of Fig. 150, and beyond this are various objects, and especially rather elaborate arrangements for water-supply, which indicate that the whole region was of special importance for either religious or political ceremonial. The plateau at the head of the steps, at the level of the top of the monument, is seen on the right of Fig. 151,* which shows also the whole extent of the court or garden. There is in the court a fairly large tank or cistern, now quite filled up with rubbish.

The southern part of the higher platform above mentioned, east of the courtyard, is enclosed by walls on the north and east sides (Fig. 152), and on a worked face in the eastern wall is a series

* A photograph taken from another point of view shows what appears to be a column or an obelisk, fallen out of the perpendicular, on this plateau. This was not noticed until the photograph was developed and printed, and was in consequence not investigated.

of four square holes like those at the top of the wall in Fig. 85, and which may well have had to do, in each case, with some arrangements for a timber roof or shelter.

The rocks and ruined monuments at the foot of the garden-court and bordering the Tarfani Wadi (Fig. 153) are among the most picturesque and bizarre in Petra. In this photograph the extraordinarily animal-like promontory in the centre has on its left the " fives court," of Fig. 85, and on its right a flight of wide but very ruinous steps leading up to the south end of the garden. To the left of the slope leading to the " fives court " there opens the elaborately quarried passage or couloir, seen from above in Fig. 154, and from below in Fig. 155. The ledge on the left of Fig. 154, which is on the level of the garden, leads round to the rough wall above the " fives court." The construction of this couloir, which gives an easy access to the steps south of the garden in Fig. 153, has involved cutting right through a solid mass of rock, and can only have been carried out for some very important reason connected with the use of this region and the monument of Fig. 106.

Continuing downwards (southwards) from Fig. 153, further steps lead out to a comparatively clear part of al Ma'aisara, directly overlooking the very literal " High Place " of Fig. 156, where the top of a somewhat isolated monument is used as an altar, approached by broad steps. On the rocks below the steps to the right are two excavations of which one is a grave and the other may be a cistern.

From our camp near the Roman Temple, one's eye was constantly caught by two enormous brown blocks, so much weathered that they seemed almost skeletons, upon the face of the western ridge of Ma'aisara looking over the Tarfani Wadi from its eastern bank. A nearer view (Fig. 157) shows that they stand on a projecting ridge of rock, picturesquely weathered into deep hollows which are of an intense deep red colour. From the side of the Turkamaniya Wadi, above which Dr. Dalman has found several very primitive " holy places," a flight of broad steps, still existing in various parts, leads up to these blocks from the east, and seems to have been constructed for that special purpose. I am sorry that time and conditions did not allow of any thorough investigation being made of this place. Fig. 158 shows some much-niched chambers behind the northern block, and shows also the front of a chamber with a door and two carefully squared windows similar to those already mentioned on al Habis. Our Arabs insisted that the place was a Madhbah—a place of sacrifice.

On the west wall of al Khubdha, north of the Florentinus tomb, there is a long series of open-fronted chambers (without architectural features, and not lending themselves well to illustration) which Brünnow has catalogued and which Dalman has subsequently arranged into a series of six " holy places," which he has described and sketched in plan, but which need not be dealt with here.

On the western slope of the Nasara Wadi, opposite the northern end of al Khubdha, there are also several places of cult. The monument of Fig. 159 (No. 657 Br.) is one of a few on which everything above the capitals, if anything ever existed, has disappeared. The chamber in this monument contains three large loculi with a fourth which has broken open right through the right-hand wall. Much trouble has been taken here with the preservation and distribution of water—a channel runs right round the top of this monument. A little further on (near No. 661 Br.) there is what appears to be a rock grave, much undercut. On examination it was found to be certainly a cemented tank, its lower part being about 10 feet by 11 feet by 5 feet, the depth to the bottom being about 8 feet. Among other signs of cult close to this occurred the recesses with idol blocks of Fig. 160.

Still further north, beyond the end of the Khubdha ridge, at the mouth of the Wadis coming down there to the level of Petra (Fig. 161, Nos. 686, 687 Br., etc.), there are many graffiti and other indications of cultural purpose. The great monuments on the Nasara massif itself do not, however, appear to belong to this class.

Among the many ruinous caves at the river level in the outer Siq the one of Fig. 162 seems clearly to have been connected with cult. It is a tripartite cave, of which whatever front ever existed has broken off. In the back-wall of the centre part is a little shrine with an idol block, having the peculiarity that a groove is cut across the back of the niche just at the top of the block (see also al Madras, Fig. 173). To the right of the central opening a narrow flight of steps (the lower part now broken away) leads up to a large recess on an upper ledge in which either an altar or a block has at one time stood. I see that, oddly enough, this cave was used as headquarters by Dr. Dalman on one of his later visits to Petra.

On a rocky promontory not far short of the Urn temple—probably the unmarked point between Nos. 777 and 778 on Brünnow's map—there is a chamber which is approached by a broad flight of steps (Fig. 165). Above these I found the small open triclinium (Fig. 167) with its central block or altar, and near it the various arrangements for water-supply which seem always to accompany places of cult.

The now well-known place of sacrifice, or Madhbah (Mizpeh), on the Obelisk ridge, to which attention was first drawn in 1882 by E. L. Wilson, stands on the highest part—the northern end—of the promontory, about 3,400 feet above sea-level and 627 feet higher than the Qasr al Bint. It can be reached readily by several more or less regular routes, and with a certain amount of rock scrambling from almost any direction (see Chapter V.).

The " place of sacrifice " (Fig. 163, No. 85a Br.) itself occupies a small and nearly level plateau close to the extremity of the Obelisk ridge. It consists essentially of what appears to be a great triclinium, about 47 feet by 21 feet, the longest dimension running from south to north. In the centre of the western side is the altar, approached by three steps, and close beside it to the south a second altar (Fig. 166), with a shallow basin 3 feet in diameter and about $4\frac{1}{2}$ inches deep, having a hole in the centre leading to a run-off channel. Further to the south, beyond the main court, there is the rain-water cistern (Fig. 168), which is roughly 10 feet by 8 feet.

Dr. Dalman has made, and published in his first volume, most careful measurements of every detail of this " holy place," and has discussed at considerable length, but without very definite results, the meaning and function of each of its parts. Here it can only be noted that the nature and method of the sacrifices offered, as well as the details of ceremonial, still remain by no means certain. It is clear, however, that any animals sacrificed must have been small. It is clear, also, that celebrations at this place can only have been witnessed by very few people, if any, besides the celebrants, for the simple reason that there is no room for others on the narrow ridge.

South of the place of sacrifice and separated from it by a great artificial corridor stand the two rough obelisks (Fig. 164) from which the ridge takes its name (see Chapter V., iii.).

Brünnow states that he found three places of sacrifice near the obelisks; I did not myself see them. In general it must be said that there do not now remain any very definite indications that the obelisk plateau itself was a place of worship, but it is hardly possible to think that the sculptors who deliberately, and with so much trouble, left the two obelisks standing as they are by cutting away large masses of surrounding rock, did so without some definite cultural object. Whether the cult of the obelisks had any connection with that of the place of sacrifice beyond them it is impossible to say. The later fortifications which now separate them probably only came into existence centuries after both were in their present position—and the same applies to the cutting of the great cross gully. This operation itself even may well have destroyed " holy places " originally connected with the obelisks, if there were any.

In every part of Petra—both at places of cult and elsewhere—graffiti of obelisks are as common as the scratched rectangles or blocks in relief. But nowhere else, with the sole exception of the tomb (Fig. 86) in the Bab al Siq, do there occur massive obelisks like these, which are comparable with the massive block tombs of Sahrij type. All the diligence and experience of Dr. Dalman and his colleagues having failed to tell us anything definite about the original Nabataean cult of which the evidences are more numerous, it is not surprising that no explanation is forthcoming as to the significance or use of these unique objects.

The actual size and shape of the obelisks themselves has been no doubt largely determined by the original dimensions of the blocks of which they are the core. The larger (western) measures about 11 feet by 7 feet at the base, and is about 23 feet in height. The base of the second is about 6½ feet by 5½ feet, and its height about 21 feet. They are due east and west of each other, and the distance between them is about 100 feet.

On the northern end of the Obelisk ridge are two normal " holy places " described, and I think discovered, by Dalman, which can be easily reached by a scramble from the direction of the theatre. More nearly on the actual northern route to the Madhbah (p. 75) stands a shrine which has some special interest, and of which Fig. 169 is a photograph. The symbolic block, about 18 inches by 7 inches, stands on a base in a deep niche, on each side of which is a rounded pilaster about 4 feet in height, surmounted by a crescent " half-moon," a symbol not occurring elsewhere, I think, in Petra.

The western or south-western route to the place of sacrifice starts from the eastern Farasa Wadi, by an ascent commencing a short distance above the Temple of Fig. 123. Not far from the start of the route are two objects of some special interest. The altar of Fig. 170 is the best preserved and most important altar to be found at Petra. Its form is shown very clearly in the photograph; its total height is nearly 6 feet. The shape of the top of the altar is not clearly defined, on account of weathering, but apparently it has horns with curved surfaces. Not far from the altar is the remarkable relief of an animal supposed to be a lion, of Fig. 206. The photograph shows clearly the water-channel which has been carefully shaped to direct its contents straight to the lion's head, with the result that the upper part of the head has been practically washed away. The object of the sculptor of this huge carving (some 15 feet by 9 feet in all) is not at all clear.

Above these objects the route continues, including in its way the ledge of Figs. 206 and 208.

Immediately beyond the Farasa Temple a flight of steps conducts to the great tank above it. This tank or cistern, the walls of which are cemented, and in which trees are now growing, is said by Wilson to be 20 feet by 60 feet, and 12 feet deep. (I have no measurements of my own.) Just beyond are the remains of the great hall of Fig. 171 (No. 246 Br.). These remains consist of three walls of what appears to have been a hall about 25 feet wide once covered over with a wagon roof. In the end- and side-walls are shallow niches, each about 6 feet by 2 feet, resembling the niches in Fig. 85, but on the ground-level instead of being high up on the wall. The shape of the roof is seen on the end-wall, and the ledge at the springing of the arch is seen on both sides. There is nothing to show that this hall was in any way connected with ceremonies which were of a religious nature, but it probably had some very important ceremonial object. The use of the arched roof and the massive masonry which has been employed in one side of the tank, as well as the design of the temple immediately below, would indicate that the whole comes from Roman rather than from Nabataean times.

The region known as al Madras, more than a mile to the south-east of the Obelisk plateau, and near the eastern limit of the white sandstone, has, for some unknown reason, always been treated as a very sacred place, and contains several places of cult sufficiently elaborate to be included as

" holy places " by Dr. Dalman, with a great number of rows of niches such as those which are notable in the Bab al Siq. One of the most remarkable of these is shown in Fig. 173 (No. 45 Br.). The sunken block symbol in the principal niche is here topped by a cross groove, as in the case of the tripartite cave of Fig. 162.

Al Madras is most easily reached by an ascent behind the Obelisk monument in the Bab al Siq, of which a great part is provided with steps.

Seen from anywhere in the site of the city the mass of Jabal Numair appears as a pointed peak, the very ideal of a " High Place " if it were only accessible. The visible peak, however, is not a cone, but the high western end of a long and high shoulder (see Fig. 11). It is due to Dr. Dalman's activity that we know now that it was certainly a holy mountain and that upon it were at least two definite places of cult. Dalman's ascent was made in 1906; I regret that none of my party in 1924 had the opportunity of repeating it. He has published a detailed description of his route, and of what he found on the mountain. Not the least interesting of his finds was a little relief, about 18 inches high, of a Roman soldier in a very lively attitude. A feature of one of the two " holy places " is a cistern formed in a natural ravine by the erection of a masonry wall at its lower end, and with provision for an arched covering, both of which features suggest Roman work, although there is nothing classical about the signs of cult.

I cannot pretend to have made an exhaustive examination of the monuments of the Ma'aisara ridges, which alone would take many days. But Fig. 172 represents a shrine with idol block carved in a huge block of sandstone, and Fig. 175 two idol niches, both photographs being taken near the head of the Wadi al Wastani.

In the extreme south of the city, at the head of the Thughra Wadi, there is an important " holy place " centred on the Sahrij tomb of Fig. 71. In the Sahrij itself there is only a small plain chamber, but on the top of it there is a hewn grave, which can be seen in Fig. 176. Fig. 174 shows on the left of the Sahrij a low chamber which has an idol niche in a corner of the back-wall. The chamber underneath the Sahrij (see Fig. 177) has three vertical loculi in each wall. To the left of this lower chamber is another, having an unusually highly decorated niche, with a hemispherical shell top. Within a few yards west of these chambers is a triclinium.

The Sahrij, with some of its accompanying chambers, is well shown in Fig. 176, taken from the side of the Snake monument. Between the latter and the Sahrij stands the great block tomb of Fig. 72 (No. 303 Br.) which contains a small plain chamber only, with two open chambers in the rock below it.

The Snake monument itself is unique among Petraean carvings. The coils of the serpent wind round a central block on the top of a plain four-square block. I know of nothing that can be said as to its probable use or significance.

This whole region stands in relation to the southern access to Petra, as does the Bab al Siq to the eastern access. It will be seen from Chapter VI. that from this point along the Thughra Wadi to the centre of the city there are hundreds of votive inscriptions and graffiti, no doubt in gratitude for safe arrival, or as request for protection on an outward journey.

I have attempted here only to indicate generally the principal cultural remains of Petra and their localities, without any idea of completeness. I have said a little more on this subject in another place, in reference to inscriptions (Chapter VI.). The cultural monuments in or near al Baidha are described in Chapter I.

CHAPTER V

THE NORTH-EASTERN REGION

I.—AL KHUBDHA

IN the preceding chapters I have given a general description of the Petraean monuments from the point of view of their general design, apart from the particular parts of the region in which they were placed. There are several places, however, of sufficient special importance to make it convenient to deal with them, and many of the monuments in them, separately. These places are: (1) al Khubdha, (2) the neighbourhood of the Siq, and (3) the Obelisk ridge, and these are described in this and the two following sections.

The great rock mass, known as al Khubdha, which forms the northern half of the eastern wall of Petra, has been mentioned in Chapter I., and is shown in the Frontispiece, Plate I., and Fig. 36, as well as in the air-plane map. Its summit is about 835 feet above the level of the Qasr al Bint.

The upper surface of al Khubdha, whether seen from the east (Frontispiece and Fig. 1) or in a nearer view from the Obelisk ridge, and still more distinctly when seen from above, appears to consist mainly of innumerable rounded masses of hard white sandstone, having often a singularly repulsive and almost offensive appearance. The air-plane survey shows the existence, among these hummocks, of several more or less level areas, some of which still carry so much vegetation as to impress a visitor with a feeling of the existence of gardens in a wilderness. In some of these clearings Musil found (1896) signs of use for religious purposes, and his discoveries have since been extended by other explorers. Finally, Dr. Dalman makes out the existence there of no less than four complete " holy places," which he describes at length.

Various ravines, provided in most cases with flights of steps in awkward places, afford access to the upper level. My colleagues, Mr. Philby and Mr. Mumm, traversed three of these routes in 1924, and the latter has enabled me to illustrate them by the use of his photographs. The route which has probably been the most important starts by the gully beyond (north-east of) the Florentinus tomb, which can either be ascended directly from the ground or by the flight of steps beside it (Fig. 178). The latter lead first to the cleared level space which is on the back of the promontory of the tomb, and which may well have been used as an assembling-place for processions. From this the route continues through the narrow artificial gangway with vertical walls through which light is falling in the photograph (Fig. 179), which can also be reached by a direct scramble up the gully on the left of the steps. The trouble which must have been taken to cut out this gangway (which is about 11 feet wide and of considerable length) is some indication of the great importance of the places of worship to which it led. The gully above the corridor is seen in Fig. 180. Mr. Mumm says that in this gully he saw more greenery than anywhere else in Petra. On the right of the gully a plateau above the " Palace " can be reached by a little scramble, and affords a good view of the theatre (Fig. 182). From this plateau a staircase (Fig. 183) forms another route upwards, which was probably the original principal route (see p. 75).

A continuation of the original gully shows on the right-hand the remains of a large water-channel.

At its upper end the gully is closed by the wall of a large reservoir (Fig. 184) which has obviously once been arched over. (The photograph shows the springing blocks of the arch, or arches, on the right.) From this point, looking over a clear space, a small chamber (No. 766 Dal.) is seen in a hummock on the left (Fig. 181), and the place of sacrifice itself among the rocks in the centre. Fig. 186 is a nearer view of the arrangement of the latter.

The actual symbol of deity seems to have been a squared block of stone, about $2\frac{1}{2}$ feet broad and 3 feet high, left in the centre of the little recess at the head of the broad steps. The large cleared court on the right of Fig. 181 must clearly have been made for some further ceremonial requirements, but is not a triclinium.

Leaving the plateau of Fig. 186, Mr. Mumm says that a curious and interesting route—not easy to be found without a guide—turns southward and finally descends to the Outer Siq by a ravine a little beyond (*i.e.*, to the eastward of) the Urn temple. Fig. 187 shows a portion of this route.

On another visit to al Khubdha Mr. Mumm varied his route by taking the staircase of Fig. 183 instead of returning to the Florentinus gully. Higher up this route leads eventually to a point near the reservoir. From the place of sacrifice, instead of returning southward or westward, the route continued northward to the highest point of al Khubdha. " Turning east, we then went through a most extraordinary bit of country. It is all white sandstone, and the whole summit-plateau is covered with domes of white rock, more or less connected, the general effect rather bald and ugly, but relieved occasionally by little garden-like places, with grass and shrubs, completely surrounded by walls of white or grey rock. There were quite a number of short spells of actual climbing. After some intricate meanderings we reached the place where you get down on the other side. The Arabs had expressed some doubt as to whether it would be practicable, and it was distinctly a *mauvais pas*, not unlike one on al Biyara—a gully of smooth worn rocks sloping gradually over to a perpendicular bit with a big pyramid of stones piled up against it. We reached the bottom at a point which was, I think, about a quarter of a mile from the north end of the tunnel " (see p. 73). The route afterwards continued down Sha'ib al Qais to the aqueduct of al Qantara (visible somewhat high up in Fig. 188), which it leaves on the right as it passes round the north and west base of al Khubdha to Nasara (Fig. 185).

Within the massif of al Khubdha on its eastern side the only place of cult of which I know lies in a small wadi west from the tunnel. This place was visited and described by Musil in 1896. Dr. Dalman ten years later gave it the name of Eagle Wadi. It contains little more than a wall-group of niches (Fig. 191), of which the most interesting is the one on the left, a tripartite shrine with an eagle in the centre part, having a block symbol in a compartment below it. The whole is shown in some detail in Fig. 192. The eagle is a very common symbol in the Madaïn Salih tombs (Chapter VII.), but appears very seldom indeed in Petra. Both Musil and Dalman give sketches (not photographs) of this shrine, both of which are somewhat incorrect in detail.

II.—THE BAB AL SIQ AND THE SIQ

It has been pointed out in an earlier chapter that the best-known approach to Petra, and certainly the line of approach most likely to be used in future, enters the city from the east, through or near Alji, and thence by the open valley now called the Bab al Siq which leads directly to the Siq itself.

At the eastern end of the Bab al Siq, about a mile from the opening of the Siq, stands the elaborate temple-like monument of al Khan (p. 43). Beside this monument are many graves and various indications that the place was one of cultural importance, which include a somewhat elaborate place of cult, with a chamber in which there are two stone sarcophagi. (I state this on the authority of several writers; I did not see the coffins myself, and this is the only case in which separate coffins have been noted.)

Between al Khan and the eastern end of the Siq there are on the northern side several series of niches with small chambers which appear to have been connected with cult of some kind. It is to be remembered that this valley must have carried caravans of travellers and traders for many centuries. The arrival at or departure from a place of security such as Petra may well have been accompanied—as it is to this day accompanied in the East—by special religious ceremonies. Fig. 189 shows two elaborate lines of niches having obviously a religious intention. One is just above the clearing on the right-hand side, and another on a vertical wall further to the left (west). This group is nearly opposite the Obelisk monument (Fig. 86), and I have already pointed out that in this neighbourhood there were a very large number of ordinary grave burials. Fig. 190 is the end of the Bab al Siq, close to the eastern opening of the Siq itself. A Sahrij block monument stands in shadow at the top of a little eminence. The masonry just over the shrubs on the right formed part of the barrage erected to divert the water of the Wadi Musa northward through a tunnel, about 6·5 metres high, and of the same breadth (Fig. 194). This tunnel (probably enough a natural feature), known as al Mudhlim, carried the water through the Wadi al Mudhlim to the head of Wadi Mataha, north of al Khubdha, and so back into the main channel of Wadi Musa in the centre of the city. Without this diversion the passage of the Siq would have become impossible during flood times in the winter. The general appearance of the Bab al Siq, seen from a little eminence to the south of it is shown in Fig. 193, which covers the region east of Fig. 189. The photograph shows two of the block monuments discussed in an earlier chapter, and shows (far to the left) the excavation for one of the few Assyrian type monuments which there are in this region (No. 15 Br.). Fig. 196 is a view of the bed of the Wadi Musa and the Bab al Siq with the three Sahrij monuments looking back towards the east.

Dr. Dalman records that he found, in connection with the places of cult in the Bab al Siq, a number of groups of small holes, arranged symmetrically, and apparently connected with the playing of some game.

Within the narrow Siq itself there are no actual places of cult (unless the Khazna was really a temple for worship), but along its walls are a large number of carved reliefs, intended, no doubt, to remind some deity of the piety of the travellers. Most of these mural reminders, here and elsewhere, are in the shape of scratched or carved obelisks, altars, or plain rectangular blocks. Out of a considerable number, the most notable is that of Fig. 197, a recess in the wall containing ten block reliefs. One of these is larger than all the rest, three (on the right) are of intermediate size, and six (on the left and close together) are much smaller. In the many cases, all over Petra, where a niche contains a single block only, it may quite probably be carved as a symbol and used in worship of some sort. But where there are three or four—or, as in this case, ten—blocks, there is no reason to think them symbols of an equal number of gods. Rather each block represents the devotion or recollection of some one person—the person who carved it, or for whom it was carved—for the god of the place. In this particular case it is not far-fetched to suppose that a family of ten (husband, wives, and sons, or father, sons, and grandsons) desired to recognise the goodness of Dusares in bringing them safely across the desert.

Fig. 195 is a similar niche containing four blocks of varying sizes.

Just beyond the Khazna, on the north side of the ravine, is the triclinium of Fig. 198 (No. 65 Br.), approached by a rough flight of steps. It consists of a chamber about 40 feet square; the " seats " on the three sides have an unusually broad rebated shelf in front of them. The coloured wall-markings in the interior, due to weathering, are unusually brilliant and picturesque. Nearly opposite this triclinium stood a somewhat elaborate shrine which was illustrated by Laborde. The spate in the Siq in 1847 (p. 53) seems to have caused the fall of the whole. The shrine contained a Greek inscription, which has since been deciphered.

From the upper end of the Eagle Gully (p. 72) one obtains a very interesting glimpse (Fig. 200) down into the Siq ravine from a height above it.

The western outlet of the Siq, flanked by a group of block monuments, is shown in Fig. 199. On the rising ground on the right of this photograph is a large chamber, of which the roof has fallen away, containing a number of recesses or loculi, which look more as if they were intended for the storage of merchandise arriving by the Siq than for graves. The doorway of this chamber, with its triangular groove decoration, has been mentioned in connection with Fig. 83.

The total length of the Siq as the crow flies is approximately 6,000 feet, but the three great loops of which it consists make the actual length much greater, and the soft gravelly bed makes walking through it very tiring. The fall from the east end of the Siq to the level of the Qasr al Bint is about 300 feet, of which the greater part is in the Siq itself. The clear breadth between walls is about 20 feet in the narrowest places, but here and there it opens out considerably. The colour and shape of its walls is so striking, and indeed so beautiful, that every step along it seems to be different from the one before it.

III.—THE OBELISK RIDGE

The Obelisk ridge, as forming both the south-western boundary of the outer Siq (Fig. 203) and the eastern wall of the city area itself (Fig. 201) is one of the most conspicuous features of Petraean scenery, as well as one of the most important regions in reference to its richness in monuments. The wall of Fig. 203 carries the theatre, beyond which it is covered by at least three tiers of monuments, mostly tombs, which have already been illustrated and discussed.

On its highest part is the notable place of sacrifice of Fig. 163, as well as remains of substantial fortification (Figs. 201 and 207), none of which are visible from below or from the site of the city. On its northern and lower end stand the two obelisks of Fig. 164, separated from the sanctuary by a great gallery running across the whole ridge. Fig. 202 is taken from near the obelisks, looking across the wall of the gallery to the ruins of the fort. Fig. 205 gives some idea of the immense amount of labour which must have been spent in carving out the gallery. It may be supposed that the gallery excavation formed, in fact, a quarry for the material required for building the fort. The actual building of the fort has been popularly attributed to Crusaders, without, I think, any sufficient justification. The work is probably much older than the twelfth century, and must belong to the time when Petra was a flourishing city, either under the Nabataeans or, more probably, the Romans (see Chapter III.).

From the point of view of Fig. 203 one of the obelisks can just be seen on the skyline across the square niche close to the left-hand edge of the ridge. It is so small, however, that it may not be visible in the reproduction. The western side of the ridge (Fig. 201) forms, with al Khubdha, the eastern wall of the city. Its lower part is covered with monuments, of which over a considerable distance there are three tiers one above the other (see Fig. 109). The monuments on the Siq side of the ridge are all Nabataean, as are the majority of those on the west side. But towards the south end of the latter, which leads to the two Farasa Wadis, there are several important monuments of the classical type, such as those of Figs. 123 and 124. The openings of the Farasa Wadis are seen in Fig. 201 on the right (south) of the Obelisk ridge, separated by the sharp-pointed mass of al Najr (see p. 13). Further south the eastern wall is continued by the Numair Wadi and the mass of Jabal Numair itself (Figs. 11 and 209).

The top of the Obelisk ridge can be reached from most directions with a little scrambling, sometimes difficult. There are, however, three recognised routes for the ascent, of which the best known is that by the Wadi Mahafir (Fig. 211), a narrow and somewhat tortuous gully starting from the outer Siq to the right (west) of the opening of the Siq itself. The ascent is made easy, as in the case of the Dair, by flights of (much worn) steps in various places, but is very steep. The most direct route from the city lies right along the back of the ridge from north to south, starting by the steps in Fig. 210, which are easily found. It is longer but not so steep as the Mahafir route, and the steepest pitches are provided with steps which are, however, not always easy to find. The third route starts from the Farasa Wadi, either by way of the lion (Fig. 206) or from a point considerably higher up the Wadi on the left. A feature of the route is the passage of the narrow ledge (Figs. 206 and 208) which seems to have struck some of the early visitors as very perilous. The Mahafir route is, of the three, the most easily traced, but all of them will be found and traversed more easily under the guidance of an Arab who knows their details.

CHAPTER VI
INSCRIPTIONS

FROM the point of view of an epigraphist, Doughty was, of course, quite right in thinking (see p. 78) that he would find more of interest at Madaïn Salih than at Petra. There are, in fact, only four or five tombs at Petra which carry any inscription at all.

The most notable is a long Nabataean inscription of five lines on the face of the Turkamaniya Tomb (Fig. 104), of which Brünnow gives a copy (p. 365), a photograph, and a translation. The inscription states that the monument and the great and little halls inside it, as well as the garden, all of which are said to be described in official documents, are sacred and dedicated to Dusares and to his Holy Throne and " to all gods." Nothing whatever is to be altered, and no one is to be buried in the tomb, or to have any use of it, except those indicated in the official papers. What the official papers may have been we do not of course know, and the inscription as it stands gives no names nor any clue to a date. In the Corpus of Semitic Inscriptions this inscription is dated in the first century B.C., which, on general grounds, would appear a very probable period. Euting, however, has expressed the opinion that it must date from a time when the Nabataean reckoning was no longer permissible, while the owners were too proud to use the Roman reckoning. This would throw its date forward to the beginning of the second century A.D., after the Roman occupation had started. Of course, Euting's opinion on such a matter is very valuable, but I hardly think the reasoning sufficiently convincing for placing this undated monument two centuries after a time when it certainly may quite possibly have been constructed.

The very ornate classical tomb of Fig. 118 carries a Latin inscription to a Roman officer, Sextius Florentinus, who has been guessed, without any very definite proof, to be an officer of the time of Hadrian or Antoninus Pius.

The monument in the outer Siq (Fig. 100), which is unique in containing quite a number of separate graves (see p. 48), carries on one side a number of scratched figures of obelisks, and contains also two short inscriptions giving the names of the persons to whom the graves belonged, but nothing more.

In al Baidha there is on a rock an engraved obelisk in low-relief, with an inscription recording that it is " the grave of Nasiru, the son of Adu," but the relief is not accompanied by any grave or monument. In the great Urn Temple (Fig. 116) there is an inscription in Greek merely painted on one wall, naming a bishop who has been identified as living about the year A.D. 447. The monument, however, was, of course, very much older than this, and may quite possibly have been used as a temple to Dusares, or possibly even as a tomb, before the Christian era, although its purely classical design would place its construction not earlier than the end of the first century A.D.

One other grave only contains an inscription of any sort. It is numbered 531 by Brünnow, but I have not been able to take a photograph of it. It is a simple corniced tomb which has never been finished; its upper part only is complete. The inscription, which is quite incomplete, simply contains two or three Nabataean words which probably represent the names of the owners, and indicate that it may have been a tomb.

An inscription in an open chamber in the Bab al Siq, which was noted by Brünnow and numbered by him 21, but which he was not able to decipher, has been read later. The place where it occurs, however, is a triclinium, not a grave. It apparently dates from about 62 B.C.

In addition to these few inscriptions on monuments, there are only one or two others which are dated at all: one (No. 41 Br.) bearing the date 70 B.C., and another in Farasa (No. 290 Br.) A.D. 20. Neither of these, however, is in a grave.

In addition to these few inscriptions definitely connected with monuments, there are a very large number of others which are purely votive and consist only of the name of the engraver, with a word equivalent to " Hail " prefixed, the whole being simply scratched on the rock. Obviously the idea of all inscriptions of this kind is exactly the same as the common Oriental idea of tying a rag to a sacred tree—the writer wishes to call the attention of his deity to himself and to the fact that he remembered him, in the hope, of course, that he himself would be remembered in turn, I have not counted the whole number of these graffiti that have been recorded. Dalman gives particulars of over ninety in his second volume. They have, of course, no very special interest. It is to be noted, however, that they are very frequently accompanied by scratched obelisks and altars, or even scratched rectangular blocks. They occur in great numbers in the " holy places " at al Madras, where one is dated 70 B.C. and dedicated to Dusares. In the " holy places " at Numair there is a very long inscription dated A.D. 20, and some thirty or forty votive inscriptions besides. In the Siyagh there are many scratched obelisks and altars, and a very great many occur along the route by which Petra has been reached from the south, on one side of the Wadi Thughra. In Farasa and in al Baidha there are also a great number of short votive inscriptions, and another group occurs near the Obelisk plateau. In a narrow ravine which he calls the Sidd el Magin (Sadd al Ma'ajin), Dr. Dalman found, and has given sketches of, a number of flat carvings of variously complicated niches, not apparently accompanied by any inscriptions, but no doubt carved with the same pious object.

In the Wadi al Dair are a certain number of inscriptions in Greek, probably of a Christian origin.

CHAPTER VII

MADAÏN SALIH AND MIDIAN

MONUMENTS carved in the rock are not uncommon in many parts of Arabia, but the only place where they occur to anything like the extent in which they are found in Petra is Madaïn Salih (al Hajar), which is on the Hajj route about 350 miles south of Petra. Our first knowledge of the tombs at Madaïn Salih is due, of course, to Charles Doughty's adventurous visit in 1876 and the descriptions and sketches which he gave in *Arabia Deserta*.

With reference to Doughty's great expedition, it is at first sight rather difficult to understand why he went to Madaïn Salih instead of making any investigations at Petra. What he himself says as to this is pretty clear:* " From thence gone up to Edom I visited Petra; and at Ma'an Settlement, which is a few miles beyond, heard of other Petra-like sculptured cliff monuments bearing many inscriptions at Madaïn Salih. Madaïn Salih—*i.e.*, cities of their reputed prophet Salih—so named by the pilgrims, being the subject of many Koran fables; but more properly, from antiquity al Hejr (as it yet is in the mouths of the country nomads), was at that time not known to Europeans.

" What might be those inscriptions ? I was unable to learn from my Arab companions, save that they were not Arabic. Interested as I was in all that pertains to Biblical research, I resolved to accept the hazard of visiting them. This was only accomplished later after more than another year's fruitless endeavours; without finding any other means I had taken the adventure of journeying thither in the great Damascus Caravan.

" Arrived at the place after three weeks' tedious riding amongst that often clamorous, mixed, and, in their religions, devout pilgrim multitude, I find Madaïn Salih to be an old ruinous sand plain with sand rock cliffs, where our encampment was pitched by a great cistern defended from the interference of Bedouins by a rude built Turkish fort, or Kella, whence it is the weary pilgrims draw to drink for themselves and their numerous camels."

Later on he says: " It was in my former coming hither (to Ma'an) I heard certainly of Madaïn Salih, of which also the villagers had spoken to me many marvellous things at Wadi Musa, supposing that I had arrived then from the southward by the Haj route. . . . Of Mahmud the Secretary, a literate person, who had been there oftentimes, I learnt more particularly of the inscriptions and images of birds in the frontispieces, and with those words Mahmud was the father of my painful travels in Arabia. Understanding that it was but ten marches' distance, I sought the means to go down thither, but the Captain of the Station thwarted me."

Half a century later the Dominican Fathers, Jaussen and Savignac, published, in connection with the French *Mission Archéologique en Arabie* (1909, etc.), very detailed descriptions of the monuments at al Hajar, accompanied by excellent photographs, which seem to make clear their relation to the Petraean monuments. It is strange that these gentlemen, while they refer to Doughty's inscriptions as published in the *C.I.S.*, never mention *Arabia Deserta*, although it had described very minutely and accurately both monuments and the country, and must surely have been before them throughout. I have not myself been able to visit Madaïn Salih, and in any case the French descriptions are so clear and complete, and their illustrations so good, that it would seem as if there were practically nothing

* *Arabia Deserta*—Preface to the second edition.

more now to be said about them. From my present point of view, however, it is quite interesting to examine the differences between the monuments at the two places. Datable inscriptions which have been deciphered at Madaïn Salih show that the whole of the monuments there must have been constructed in the first century of our era. One apparently belongs to the year 1 B.C., and one to the year A.D. 1, while others are as late as A.D. 72. The total number of monuments is sixty-five or sixty-six—that is to say, from one-tenth to one-twelfth of the total number of monuments at Petra. They contain examples of all the principal Petraean types, with the exception of the block monuments (Sahrij), and those very old ones which have only rectilinear decoration, and with the entire exception also of monuments of classical type. The differences between individual monuments in their architectural details have been examined with extraordinary diligence by the French Fathers, aided by the fact that the condition of the monuments in general is very much better than that of the generality of the Petraean monuments, owing perhaps largely to their very much later average date. One cannot look over the drawings of the southern monuments without coming to the conclusion that they are based entirely on Petraean models. There are, oddly enough, a number of small differences partly due to intention, but largely, one would imagine, to imperfect recollection. Of intentional differences, the chief is no doubt that the great majority of the Madaïn Salih monuments have on their faces a cartouche intended for an inscription, and in about half the monuments the inscription itself actually exists and has been copied and deciphered. There is not a single one of the Petraean monuments, so far as I know, which contains on its front any provision for an inscription, and, as Chapter VI. explains, there are only four or five of them which carry any inscription at all.

In most of the tombs of the Assyrian type at Madaïn Salih there is a straight moulding across the top of the upper row of crowsteps, joining them together. I have only found this detail in one single case at Petra. In all these cases similarly the number of steps in each little gable is five, whereas in Petra it is always four. In the Assyrian originals it is three. In one case (C. 14) the two rows of crowsteps are placed close together, one above the other, and in one case the number of steps is different in the two rows, being four in one and five in the other. There are one or two examples of tombs having a cornice with a row of small steps above it, instead of the normal immense half-gables. This occurs only once at Petra, so far as I have discovered, in the case of a Sahrij which is unfinished. I do not make out with any certainty that there is even a single one of the Madaïn Salih monuments in which there is the longitudinal groove over the doorway which is so extremely common in the early monuments at Petra. As a whole, however, the doorways at Madaïn Salih are much more decorative than those at Petra, and in very many cases the pediment is surmounted by a bird, presumably an eagle, which again is a feature which I do not remember as occurring in any case at Petra. Classical acrotères on the architraves at the doorways are very common, but at Petra these never appear to occur except in monuments of classical design. In a very large number of the corniced monuments also, of the more decorated type, the pilasters are surmounted only with a plain-angled capital. Where this has not been used the capitals are obviously based on the Nabataean type, although their proportions are somewhat markedly different, and, as the French investigators point out, differ very much among themselves. In Petra there are twelve of the most decorative type of corniced monuments having an attic between two cornices—that is to say, about one-fortieth of the whole number (520) belonging to this class. In Madaïn Salih there are, however, twenty-two monuments of this type out of forty-seven altogether, or nearly one-half. There is only one example of a double-cornice tomb having a quasi-second order in the attic and resembling in this respect the Turkamaniya tomb at Petra. This tomb at Madaïn Salih is identified as belonging to A.D. 63. If my examination of the published particulars is correct, every one of the monuments which is definitely described as a tomb by an inscription contains in its interior chamber some definite provision for burials. It may be reasonably assumed that the chambers which are still found bare would have been provided with graves of some sort later on when they were actually required as tombs.

It is interesting to notice that although the Madaïn Salih monuments contain examples of early and late Nabataean designs, there is no chronological relation between their date in the first century and their design. Plain monuments, such as B. 10 and E. 16, having a single row of crowsteps only, are dated A.D. 34 and A.D. 74; C. 17, a double row of crowsteps, A.D. 16; C. 14, another double row, A.D. 60; while single- and double-corniced tombs date from 1 B.C. and A.D. 11 onwards to A.D. 75. One very plain single-row tomb without any pilasters is as late as A.D. 72.

It is very specially notable that while these monuments of the first century A.D. show us that every one of the Nabataean types had been known at that time, there is not a single example of a classical monument to be found, which gives us a fair presumption that the classical type at Petra does not date earlier than the Roman occupation in A.D. 106.

No case of a chamber is reported as being a triclinium; in fact, the only indication of cult which the French Fathers describe at al Hajar is the Diwan, apparently a sacred cave, beside which are scratched on the rocks just such votive inscriptions with obelisks, etc., as have been found at Petra.

It is worthy of note that at Khuraiba (Jaussen's Hereibeh and Doughty's Al Khreyby) the rock tombs are of an entirely different type, being merely rectangular hollows, cut in a cliff face, into which the bodies were pushed. The inscriptions in these cases are no longer Nabataean, but Libyanitic or Himyaritic. Beside some of these tombs are rock carvings of monsters, roughly like front views of Assyrian lions. The language and the monsters together seem to indicate that the Nabataean kingdom stopped short at Madaïn Salih. It is also notable that within a very few miles of Madaïn Salih Jaussen found the ruins of what must have been a large Roman temple. No walls were standing, but the bases of columns were visible, and he made out clearly the general arrangement of the whole and gives a diagram of what the buildings must have been. These appear to correspond more or less to the Roman ruins on the Dair plateau and to the many indications of large Roman buildings which are still to be seen on the site of the city of Petra itself.

MIDIAN

On his journey to Midian of 1879, Burton visited and described Madiama, which he calls " evidently the capital of Madyan Proper, ranking after Petra." The place is in ruins, but " in one point it is still what it was, a chief station upon the highway, then Nabati, now Moslem, which led to the Ghor or Wadi Araba."*

Madiama is in the shoreland of Midian on the Gulf of Akaba, about thirty miles above the mouth of the Gulf. Burton found there tombs entirely of the Petraean type. His illustration on p. 103 is of a corniced monument without the cornice, but with a frieze of small crowsteps below the great half-gables. On p. 107 he pictures a normal Assyrian type of monument, with two rows of crowsteps, and beside it another with three rows. He speaks of one (p. 109) " flanked by pilasters with ram's-horn capitals " (probably the ordinary Nabataean), " barbarous forms of Ionic connected by three sets of triglyphs." It would appear that the rock carvers of Madiama, like those of Madaïn Salih many miles further south, have based their designs on those of Petra, but have used their discretion as to details in a way which would have shocked the rigidly conventional Petraean workers.

* Burton, *The Land of Midian revisited*, 1879, Vol. I., pp. 102 *et seq.*

CHAPTER VIII

UNSOLVED QUESTIONS AT PETRA

PETRA remains in reality, in spite of the work which has been done upon it, a riddle very largely unsolved. The first serious question about it, if it could be undertaken, would be as to the nature, customs and particularly the religious beliefs of the original inhabitants, quite possibly earlier inhabitants than the Nabataeans. Naturally, we can only get this information by excavation, and so far the authorities have not permitted any digging at all to be done. The Arabs themselves, of course, consider that the diggers are looking for treasure, and unfortunately, when they see that the diggers do not find any, they are not satisfied that the treasure does not exist, but have remained convinced in many cases that the diggers, having discovered where the treasure is, have sufficient " white magic " about them to convey the treasure to themselves afterwards, wherever they may be. Besides this popular and merely superficial fear of losing treasure, the authorities themselves, on what they consider religious grounds, are very averse from allowing the soil to be interfered with. I trust, however, that in future years persuasion may be more effective than it has been hitherto.

Excavation cannot fail to explain many matters to us in connection with the rites and ceremonies both of the places of sacrifice and of the places of feasting, which are so extremely numerous in Petra.

In spite of the deep consideration which has been given to the subject by Dr. Dalman and his colleagues, it must be said that our ideas as to the religious ceremonials of the Nabataeans and their predecessors remain very vague indeed. We do not know whether on the altar they had an image or not, and we do not know whether the offerings were burnt offerings or were animal offerings at all; in fact, it is clear that we know nothing whatever of any certainty about these most interesting matters beyond what we can make out by the analogy of Jewish and other Semitic worship which we get in the Hebrew histories.

Mr. Doughty found flint implements at Ma'an on the desert, and similar relics have been found during the last three years at numerous sites between that place and Shaubak, while one of our visitors in 1923, Mr. Oscar Raphael of the British Museum, found two palaeolithic implements quite on the surface in Petra itself, near the place where the Wadi Nasara runs into the Wadi Musa (Figs. 61 and 62). The ordinary surface findings in Petra just now are only Roman pottery shards and coins of no particular interest.

A second matter of investigation which only requires time, personnel, and patience, is the determination of the actual purpose of the various chambers. This means certainly an entry into and examination of every individual chamber among all the hundreds that exist. The earlier explorers were satisfied simply to call them all tombs. We know from such examination as we have been able to make that a great many of them were not tombs, but what they were in many cases is still quite uncertain. I have in Chapter IV. mentioned the forms in which definite graves appear in the chambers, but apart from these there must be a great many cases in which there are graves in some of the chambers entirely filled up with debris probably lying on the top of the stones which cover the graves, but not to be identified in any way until the floor of the chambers can be cleared. It

M

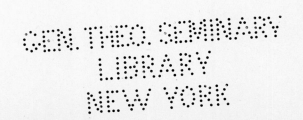

would be a long piece of work to get this done, but it really is a necessary piece of work to get at the meaning of the Petraean monuments.

It may very well prove that the investigation of the great ravine, of which the existence is made known for the first time by the Air-Plane Survey (Plate III.), turns out to be the most interesting piece of work which still remains to be done at Petra.

The existence of upper chambers has, I confess, also been a puzzle to me. Very few of them can be entered except by the help of a ladder, and it would be very interesting indeed to know what relation in different cases they bear to the large and immediately accessible chambers below them.

Another point on which I personally as an engineer am particularly interested, and as to which I have as yet been unable to form any definite opinion, is the nature of the tools by which the actual work of carving the enormous monuments was carried out, and the way in which they were used. I can quite suppose that the use of the very simple rectilinear designs of what appear to be the most ancient of the façades may have been determined by the fact that they were more easy to carve than the later more elaborate ones, and, therefore, that the elaboration of the designs has proceeded *pari passu* with the elaboration of the tools and the methods available.

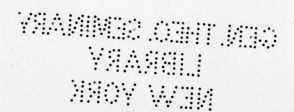

PLATE 1.

"OBLIQUE" LOOKING UP THE SITE OF THE CITY FROM NORTH TO SOUTH BETWEEN THE WESTERN RANGE (ON RIGHT) AND THE KHUBDHA MASS ON LEFT, WITH THE OUTLET OF THE SIQ. THE NASARA ROCKS ARE IN THE CENTRE IN THE FOREGROUND.

PLATE 2.

"OBLIQUE" OF J. HARUN (MT HOR) TAKEN FROM NORTH TO SOUTH OVER THE MOUNTAINS OF THE WESTERN WALL.

PLATE 3.

"OBLIQUE" SHOWING A HITHERTO UNKNOWN WADI TO THE SOUTH EAST OF THE CITY. (SEE PAGES 19 AND 82).

FIG. 1.

DISTANT VIEW OF THE
PETRA RIDGES, WITH
J. HARUN, FROM THE
VILLAGE OF ALJI.

FIG. 2.

THE PORPHYRY RIDGE
ACROSS THE LOWER
SIYAGH.

FIG. 3.

GROUP OF ARABS AT
QASR AL BINT.

FIG. 4.

MA'AN.

FIG. 5.

THE CITY AREA WITH
THE EASTERN WALL
AND J. NUMAIR.
THE DESERT UPLANDS
IN THE BACKGROUND.

FIG. 6.

THE MATAHA
AND NASARA
WADIS, FROM NEAR
THE "PALACE".

FIG. 7.

THE WADI TURKAMANIYA,
LOOKING NORTH.

FIG. 8.

THE WADI TURKAMANIYA,
WITH AL NAJR AND THE
WHITE RIDGE OF NASARA.

FIG. 9.

THE THREE WADIS OF THE
MA'AISARA REGION, FROM
ABOVE THE QASR AL BINT.

FIG. 11.

MOUTH OF THE WADI
FARASA AND J. NUMAIR.

FIG. 10.   UPPER PART OF THE
EAST WADI FARASA.

FIG. 12.   PLATEAU ON J. HARUN.

JUNCTION OF WADI THUGHRA
WITH THE SIYAGH.

THE CITY AREA FROM NORTH
TO SOUTH. NASARA IN
FOREGROUND. IN THE WESTERN
RIDGE AL BIYARA ABOVE
AL HABIS WITH THE EXTREME
UPPER PART OF AL BARRA
SHOWING ABOVE IT, J. HARUN
IN DISTANCE.

WADI THUGHRA. VIEW TO
THE NORTH-EAST FROM NEAR
THE SOUTHERN WATERSHED.

FIG. 16.

A LOWER REACH OF
THE SIYAGH.

FIG. 17.

AL BIYARA BEHIND THE
OPENING OF THE SIYAGH.

FIG. 18.

LOOKING DOWN THE SIYAGH
FROM MA'AISARA.
AL HABIS ON THE LEFT,
WITH BIYARA BEHIND IT.

NORTHWARD VIEW FROM AL HABIS.

FIG. 19.

PANORAMA LOOKING SOUTHWARDS FROM THE DAIR PLATEAU.
THE PINNACLES OF AL BARRA ON THE LEFT.—J. HARUN BEHIND.

FIG. 20.

FIG. 21.   MOSQUE ON J. HARUN—
("AARON'S TOMB.")

FIG. 23.   VIEW FROM J. HARUN.

FIG. 22.   GULLY ON THE ASCENT OF J. HARUN.

FIG. 24.

AL HABIS AND AL
BIYARA-OPENING OF
SIYAGH ON RIGHT.

FIG. 25.

S.E. VIEW ACROSS SITE OF
PETRA FROM AL BIYARA.

FIG. 26.

WESTERN VIEW FROM
AL BIYARA.

FIG. 28.

OPENING OF THE
QATTAR AL DAIR.

FIG. 27.   IN THE WADI AL DAIR.

FIG. 29.

LEDGE ON SOUTHERN
END OF AL BIYARA.

FIG. 31.

COULOIR IN THE ASCENT
OF AL BIYARA.

FIG. 30.   EASTERN VIEW FROM THE WADI AL DAIR.

FIG. 32.

FOOT OF THE WADI AL DAIR.

FIG. 33.

MA'AISARAT AL WASTANI.

FIG. 34

EASTWARD VIEW
FROM THE DAIR
PLATEAU (AL
KHUBDHA AND
THE DESERT).

FIG. 35.

WHITE SANDSTONE
ABOVE NASARA.

FIG. 36.   EASTERN WALL FROM CAMP. RUINS OF ARCH IN SHADOW. (SUNSET).

FIG. 37.   LOOKING DOWN WADI HURAIMIYA FROM SOUTH.   FIG. 38.   OUTSIDE THE ENTRANCE TO THE
                                                                      SIQ OF AL BARID (CLASSICAL MONUMENT).

FIG. 39.

AL NAJR.

FIG. 40.

AL NAJR FROM
TURKAMANIYA WADI.

FIG. 41.

IDOL BLOCKS—
HIGH PLACE OF AL NAJR.

FIG. 42.

HIGH PLACE
AT AL NAJR.

FIG. 43.

CULTURAL REMAINS
TO THE NORTH
OF AL NAJR.

FIG. 44.

CULTURAL REMAINS
TO THE NORTH
OF AL NAJR.

FIG. 45.

TOMBS IN WHITE
SANDSTONE—FROM
AL NAJR.

FIG. 46.

BIRKA BELOW ALJI.

FIG. 47.

HIGH PLACE ON RAS
AL KHAUR ROAD,
(UMM SAIKUN).

FIG. 48.

SHAIB QAIS FROM SOUTH.

FIG. 49.

STIBADIUM IN
SHAIB QAIS
(WU'AIRA DISTRICT).

FIG. 50.

RUINS OF AL WU'AIRA.

FIG. 51.

BAIDHA PLAIN.

FIG. 52.

BAIDHA RIDGE.

FIG. 53.

HIGH PLACE AT ABU RUQ'A.

FIG. 54.

IN THE WHITE SANDSTONE
AT AL BAIDHA.

FIG. 55.   ENTRANCE TO THE SIQ OF AL BARID.

FIG. 56.   TEMPLE IN THE SIQ AL BARID.

FIG. 57.

HIGH PLACE
AT AL BARID.

FIG. 58.

SABRA VALLEY.

FIG. 59.

THEATRE AT SABRA.

FIG. 60.   SABRA—LOOKING UP.

FIG. 61.

FIG. 62.

FLINT IMPLEMENTS FOUND AT PETRA.

64.   A CAVE WITH MANY NICHES
IN AL SIYAGH.

FIG. 63.   LINE OF CAVES BESIDE A PLACE OF CULT IN AL SIYAGH.

FIG. 65.   ROCK GRAVE, WITH COVER STONES IN PLACE.

FIG. 66.

GROUP OF RUINOUS
MONUMENTS IN AL NASARA.

FIG. 67.

CORBELLED RECESS FOR
COFFIN, WITH SYMBOLIC
NOTCHES. (AL HABIS).

FIG. 68.

GROUP   OF   BLOCK
MONUMENTS BESIDE THEATRE
IN OUTER SIQ.

FIG. 69   SAHRIJ IN BAB-AL-SIQ.

FIG. 70   SAHRIJ IN THE OUTER SIQ.

FIG. 71.

SAHRIJ AMONG THE
SOUTHERN GRAVES.

FIG. 73.   TWO TOMBS WITH RECTILINEAR DECORATION—WADI AL DAIR.

FIG. 74.   TOMB WITH RECTILINEAR DECORATION IN COURT BEHIND AL HABIS.

G. 72.   SERPENT MONUMENT AND BLOCK TOMB - SOUTHERN GRAVES.

FIG 75.

BRONZE MODEL ASSYRIAN TOWER—BRITISH MUSEUM.

FIG. 77.

PANEL FROM ASSYRIAN LION HUNT—BRITISH MUSEUM.

FIG. 76.

RECTILINEAR ORNAMENT—EGYPTIAN SARCOPHAGUS—
BRITISH MUSUEM.

FIG. 78.

MODEL OF HOUSE OR FORT—BRITISH MUSEUM.

FIG. 79.

RECTILINEAR TOMB
WADI THUGHRA.

FIG. 80.

CORNICED TOMB BESIDE
LIVING CHAMBER
(COURT OF AL HABIS).

FIG. 81.

MUCH WEATHERED RECTILINEAR
DECORATION (WEST SIDE OF
OBELISK RIDGE).

FIG. 82.   CHOKED UP MONUMENT—UNUSUAL ORNAMENT.

FIG. 83.   DOORWAY OF STOREHOUSE OR SERAI—OUTER SIQ.

FIG. 84.   INTERIOR OF ANOTHER STOREHOUSE OR SERAI—OUTER SIQ.

FIG. 85. (PROBABLY) BACK WALL OF A COVERED COURT—AL MA'AISARA.

FIG. 86.

TOMB WITH OBELISKS AND
CLASSICAL TOMB—BAB-AL-SIQ.

FIG. 88.

TYPICAL ASSYRIAN MONUMENT WITH
DOUBLE CROWSTEP FRIEZE (OUTER SIQ).

FIG. 87.   TWO ARCH-TOPPED GRAVES.

FIG. 89.   ASSYRIAN TYPE MONUMENTS IN OUTER SIQ, BESIDE THEATRE.

FIG. 90.

ASSYRIAN TYPE MONUMENTS IN
OUTER SIQ, EAST SIDE.

FIG. 91.

GROUP OF MONUMENTS
WITH DOUBLE FRIEZE,
INCLUDING FIG. 88.

FIG. 92.

MONUMENTS ON THE FOOT OF
AL BIYARA—WADI THUGHRA.
(DOUBLE LINE OF GRAVES
PRACTICALLY DESTROYED AT FOOT).

FIG. 93.   MONUMENTS IN WADI AL DAIR.

FIG. 95.   A DOUBLE STORY GRAVE—AL BARRA.

FIG. 94.   ASSYRIAN TYPE MONUMENTS ON MA'AISARA.

FIG. 96.

PLAIN CORNICED MONUMENT,
MUCH WEATHERED—NEAR AL NASARA.

FIG. 97.

CORNICED MONUMENT WITH
PRIMITIVE PILASTERS.

FIG. 98.

GRAVE WITH RECTILINEAR
DECORATION AND LINTEL NOTCHES.
AN IDOL NICHE ON LEFT OF DOORWAY.

FIG. 99.   GROUP OF ASSYRIAN TYPE TOMBS NEAR MOUTH OF SIQ.

FIG. 100.   MONUMENT WITH DOUBLE CORNICE, (OUTER SIQ).

FIG. 101.   MUCH WEATHERED CORNICED MONUMENT, WITH IDOL NICHE
(WEST WALL OF OBELISK RIDGE).

FIG. 102.

DECORATED DOUBLE CORNICED
MONUMENT—AL NASARA.

FIG. 103.

DOUBLE STORY MONUMENT IN OUTER SIQ.

FIG. 104.

TOMB WITH NABATAEAN INSCRIPTION (WADI TURKAMANIYA

FIG. 105.

WEATHERED CORNICED
TOMB, REMARKABLE
FOR ITS BEAUTIFUL
COLOURING.

FIG. 106.

DECORATED DOUBLE
CORNICED MONUMENT
AT HEAD OF COURT
IN AL MA'AISARA.

FIG. 107.

DECORATED DOUBLE CORNICED TRICLINIUM—AL NASARA.

FIG. 108.   REMARKABLE WEATHERING EFFECTS, AND FALLEN FACADE—
WEST SIDE OF OBELISK RIDGE.

G. 109.   THREE TIERS OF MONUMENTS—
WEST SIDE OF OBELISK RIDGE.

FIG. 110.   LINE OF FOUR DOUBLE CORNICED MONUMENTS ABOVE WADI AL WASTA.

FIG. 111.   KHAZNA IN THE SIQ.

FIG. 112.   "LION" TRICLINIUM, WITH IDOL IN NICHE ON LEFT—
                 NEAR FOOT OF WADI AL DAIR.

FIG. 113.   THE "PALACE" ("TROIS ÉTAGES").

FIG. 114.   THE DAIR.

FIG. 115.

ON THE NORTH
SIDE OF THE
NASARA BLOCK.

FIG. 116.   THE URN TEMPLE—OUTER SIQ.

FIG. 117.   CORINTHIAN MONUMENT (BESIDE THE "PALACE").

FIG. 118.

TOMB OF SEXTIUS
FLORENTINUS.

FIG. 119.   TRICLINIUM CONTAINING A GRAVE.
(THREE URNS) WADI AL DAIR.

FIG. 120.   ROMAN VASE.

FIG. 121.   KHAZNA.

FIG. 122.   DECORATED CLASSICAL TOMB—WESTERN WALL OF OBELISK RIDGE.

FIG. 123.   FARASA TEMPLE.

FIG. 124.   CLASSICAL TEMPLE OR TOMB, WITH SHALLOW NICHES—
                            NEAR FARASA WADI.

FIG. 125.   URN ON THE DAIR.

FIG. 127.   ARCH IN QASR AL BINT (ROMAN).

FIG. 126.   QASR AL BINT (ROMAN).

FIG. 128.

CHAMBER WITH FLUTED
COLUMNS—FARASA.

FIG. 129.

TOMB OF THE STATUES—
FARASA.

FIG. 130.

RUINS OF TRIPLE
ARCHWAY (ROMAN).

FIG. 131.   ROMAN THEATRE.

FIG. 133.   CAMP AT QASR AL BINT WITH
CAVES IN AL HABIS BEHIND.

FIG. 132.   COLUMBARIUM.

FIG. 134. OPENING OF SIYAGH. IN FOREGROUND ROMAN ALTAR BESIDE
QASR AL BINT. WINDOWED CHAMBER IN THE WALL OF AL HABIS.

FIG. 135. INTERIOR OF CHAMBER WITH WINDOWS.

FIG 136. A SECOND (UNFINISHED) CHAMBER WITH WINDOWS (AL HABIS).

FIG. 137.   OPENING OF SIYAGH, ON LEFT THE N. END OF AL HABIS WITH WINDOWED CHAMBER AND LEDGE.

FIG. 138.   SQUARE COURT BEHIND AL HABIS BEYOND WHICH IS THE SACELLUM OF FIG. 139.
IN THE CORNER A CHAMBER WITH A MANGER GRAVE,   AND ROUND THE WALLS
THREE DWELLING CHAMBERS.

FIG. 139.

SACELLUM BEHIND AL HABIS. IN THE BACKGROUND THE WALL OF AL BIYARA ON THE FAR SIDE OF THE THUGHRA WADI.

FIG. 140.

WINDOWED CHAMBER AND OTHER PLACES BESIDE THE SACELLUM.

FIG. 141.

CHAMBERED BLOCK BEHIND AL HABIS WITH A NUMBER OF NICHES, AND A SIDE PLATFORM REACHED BY STEPS.

FIG. 142.　　　　　A HOLY PLACE IN THE SIYAGH.

FIG. 143.　　　PROJECTING ROCK IN SIYAGH WITH
CAVE CARRYING NUMEROUS NICHES,
PROBABLY A PLACE OF CULT.

FIG. 144.　　　THE ROCK OF FIG. 143 SEEN FROM ABOVE.

FIG. 145

ANOTHER VIEW OF THE
TERRACES OF FIG. 144.

FIG. 146.

A ROCK GRAVE HIDDEN
AMONG THE SHRUBS AT
THE FOOT OF FIG. 143

FIG. 147.

THE DAIR PLATEAU (THE
URN VISIBLE OVER RIDGE).

FIG. 148.

ON MA'AISARA
(AN OVERGROWN SACELLUM).

FIG. 149.

COURT (CONTAINING
CISTERN) IN FRONT
OF MONUMENT, FIG. 106.

FIG. 150.

STIBADIUM FORMING PART
OF PLACE OF CULT ABOVE 149.

FIG. 151.

GENERAL VIEW (ACROSS WADI
AL TARFANI) OF FIGS. 106, 85
AND 152 (MA'AISARA).

FIG. 152.

EXCAVATIONS OF PROBABLY
ROOFED COURT EAST OF
NO. 149.

FIG. 153.

SOUTHERN APPROACH
TO 85 AND 149.

FIG. 154.

AT FOOT OF 149 ;
COULOIR ROUND 85.

FIG. 155.

LOWER END OF
COULOIR IN 154.

FIG. 156.

HIGH PLACE ON
MA'AISARA, BELOW 149.

FIG. 157.

WEATHERED MASSES OF
RED SANDSTONE ABOVE
WADI AL TARFANI.

FIG. 158.

PLACE OF CULT BEHIND
WADI AL TARFANI.

FIG. 159.

WEATHERED MONUMENT
FORMING PART OF PLACE
OF CULT—NASARA.

FIG. 160.

IDOLS IN NICHES
NEAR NO. 159.

FIG. 161.

HEAD OF WADI MATAHA.

FIG. 162.

TRIPLE CAVE WITH SIGNS
OF CULT IN OUTER SIQ.

FIG. 163.   THE PLACE OF SACRIFICE ON THE OBELISK RIDGE.

FIG. 164.   THE OBELISKS.

FIG. 165.

PLACE OF CULT
IN OUTER SIQ.

FIG. 166.

ALTAR AT HIGH
PLACE (FIG 163).

FIG. 167.

ALTAR AT FIG. 165.

FIG. 168.   CISTERN AT HIGH PLACE (FIG. 163)

FIG. 169.   MOON SHRINE (OBELISK RIDGE).

FIG. 170.   ALTAR (ABOVE FARASA).

FIG. 171.

END OF ROMAN HALL
(ABOVE FARASA).

FIG. 172.

SHRINE WITH IDOL—
TOP OF WADI AL WASTA.

FIG. 173.

HOLY PLACE
IN AL MADRAS.

FIG. 175.

IDOL NICHES—
WADI AL WASTA.

FIG. 176.

SNAKE MONUMENT—
LOOKING DOWN TO
SAHRIJ FIG. 174.

FIG. 174.   SAHRIJ NEAR SOUTHERN WATERSHED.

FIG. 177.   ANOTHER VIEW OF SAHRIJ.

FIG. 178.   STAIRWAY BESIDE FLORENTINUS TOMB.

FIG. 179.   ON THE ASCENT OF AL KHUBDHA.

FIG. 180.   ON THE ASCENT OF AL KHUBDHA.

FIG. 183.   HOLY PLACE ON AL KHUBDHA.

FIG. 181.   ON THE ASCENT OF AL KHUBDHA.

FIG. 184.   ARCHED RESERVOIR, AL KHUBDHA.

FIG. 182.   THE THEATRE FROM AL KHUBDHA.

FIG. 186.

PLACE OF SACRIFICE,
AL KHUBDHA.

FIG. 185.   N.W. DESCENT FROM AL KHUBDHA.

FIG. 187.   SOUTHERN DESCENT FROM AL KHUBDHA.

FIG. 188.

AL QANTARA FROM
N.W. (AQUEDUCT).

FIG. 189.

BAB-AL-SIQ.—
HOLY PLACES.

FIG. 190.

BARRAGE AT EASTERN
END OF SIQ.

FIG. 191.

HOLY PLACE IN
THE EAGLE GULLY.

FIG. 192.   EAGLE SHRINE.

FIG. 194.   THE TUNNEL (AL MUDHLIM).

FIG. 193.   BAB-AL-SIQ – SAHRIJ MONUMENTS.

FIG. 195.   4 BLOCK NICHE IN THE SIQ.

FIG. 196.   BAB-AL-SIQ, WITH SAHRIJ MONUMENTS.

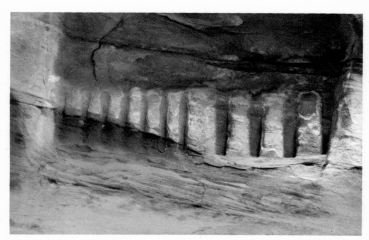

FIG. 197.   10 BLOCK NICHE IN THE SIQ.

FIG. 198.   TRICLINIUM OPPOSITE TO THE KHAZNA.

FIG. 199.   WESTERN OPENING OF THE SIQ—
GROUP OF BLOCK TOMBS.

FIG. 200.   LOOKING DOWN INTO THE SIQ FROM
THE HEAD OF THE EAGLE GULLY.

FIG. 201.

WESTERN FACE OF
OBELISK RIDGE AND
OPENING OF WADI FARASA.

FIG. 202.

RUINED FORT BESIDE
THE PLACE OF SACRIFICE,
FROM THE OBELISKS.

FIG. 203.

OUTER SIQ, THEATRE
AND OBELISK RIDGE.

FIG. 204.

INTERIOR OF
A STOREHOUSE
(OUTER SIQ).

FIG 205.

ARRIED WALLS OF
E COULOIR CROSSING
E OBELISK RIDGE.

FIG. 206.   THE LION MONUMENT—
FARASA LEDGE AT TOP OF PHOTOGRAPH.

FIG. 207.   TOWER OF FORT, FIG. 202.

FIG. 208.   THE LEDGE ACROSS THE ROCK ABOVE THE LION OF FIG. 206.

FIG. 210.

FOOT OF WESTERN ASCENT
TO PLACE OF SACRIFICE.

FIG. 209.   OPENING OF WADI NUMAIR—
JABAL NUMAIR ON RIGHT.

FIG. 211.   LOOKING DOWN WADI
MEHAFIR ACROSS THE CITY.

INDEX

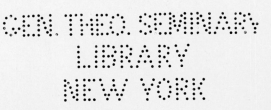

PRINTED IN GREAT BRITAIN BY BILLING AND SONS, LTD., GUILDFORD AND ESHER